**New Directions for
Community Colleges**

Arthur M. Cohen
EDITOR-IN-CHIEF

Richard L. Wagoner
ASSOCIATE EDITOR

Gabriel Jones
MANAGING EDITOR

P9-CKD-730

Marginalized
Students

Elizabeth M. Cox
Jesse S. Watson
EDITORS

Number 155 • Fall 2011
Jossey-Bass
San Francisco

LB
2328
.N48
No.155

MARGINALIZED STUDENTS
Elizabeth M. Cox, Jesse S. Watson (eds.)
New Directions for Community Colleges, no. 155

Arthur M. Cohen, Editor-in-Chief
Richard L. Wagoner, Associate Editor
Gabriel Jones, Managing Editor

NEW DIRECTIONS FOR COMMUNITY COLLEGES (ISSN 0194-3081, electronic ISSN 1536-0733) is part of The Jossey-Bass Higher and Adult Education Series and is published quarterly by Wiley Subscription Services, Inc., A Wiley Company, at Jossey-Bass, 989 Market Street, San Francisco, CA 94103-1741. Periodicals Postage Paid at San Francisco, California, and at additional mailing offices. POSTMASTER: Send address changes to New Directions for Community Colleges, Jossey-Bass, 989 Market Street, San Francisco, CA 94103-1741.

SUBSCRIPTIONS cost $89.00 for individuals and $259.00 for institutions, agencies, and libraries in the United States. Prices subject to change.

EDITORIAL CORRESPONDENCE should be sent to the Editor-in-Chief, Arthur M. Cohen, at the Graduate School of Education and Information Studies, University of California, Box 951521, Los Angeles, CA 90095-1521. All manuscripts receive anonymous reviews by external referees.

New Directions for Community Colleges is indexed in CIJE: Current Index to Journals in Education (ERIC), Contents Pages in Education (T&F), Current Abstracts (EBSCO), Ed/Net (Simpson Communications), Education Index/Abstracts (H. W. Wilson), Educational Research Abstracts Online (T&F), ERIC Database (Education Resources Information Center), and Resources in Education (ERIC).

Microfilm copies of issues and articles are available in 16mm and 35mm, as well as microfiche in 105mm, through University Microfilms Inc., 300 North Zeeb Road, Ann Arbor, MI 48106-1346.

CONTENTS

EDITORS' NOTES

Berta Vigil Laden's (2004) edited volume *New Directions for Community Colleges: Serving Minority Populations* acts as the cornerstone for this volume. The collected chapters put forth by Vigil Laden cataloged a growing conversation about diversity in community colleges. We are taking advantage of that space and offering the next iteration of this conversation regarding diversity, minority populations, and those whose voices have been marginalized. For all of the authors in this volume, diversity means more than race and ethnicity. Community colleges are the postsecondary home for immigrants, adult students, and others who see the American community college as *the* institution providing access and opportunity. Thus, in today's college environments, diversity also includes attributes such as gender, age, physical ability, sexual orientation, and academic ability. "Community colleges can truly become democracy's college by assuring that all groups have a central place in the organizational life of the institution" (Rhoads & Valadez, 1996, p. 217).

The American community college has been known by many names, including junior college, city college, technical institute, and even democracy's college. "People's college" (Cohen & Brawer, 2008) resonates with us and adds to the foundation of this volume. The title of people's college leads us to think of a place where anyone can be accepted and educated. Statistics bear this out, as community colleges serve 46 percent of all undergraduates in the United States, including large numbers of minority student populations—55 percent of Hispanic undergraduates, and 46 percent of Black and Asian/Pacific Islander undergraduates (American Association of Community Colleges, retrieved September 25, 2008). As Vigil Laden (2004) noted, "At the beginning of the twenty-first century, community colleges continue to exemplify historical American core values of providing educational access and opportunity to all citizens and residents" (p. 1).

Our principal intent for this volume is to examine how diverse and marginalized populations are situated within American community colleges. The chapters examine various student groups, which one would expect, but also included is a chapter giving voice to the marginalization felt by a group of faculty. It is through this expanded view that our second purpose of the volume is situated—to push the boundaries of our understanding of the terms *diverse* and *marginalized*. Gone are the days when the term *diversity* may have been used to solely signify the color of one's skin or gender.

This volume is useful for a variety of audiences and, we believe, particularly for those working with marginalized groups on community college

NEW DIRECTIONS FOR COMMUNITY COLLEGES, no. 155, Fall 2011 © 2011 Wiley Periodicals, Inc.
Published online in Wiley Online Library (wileyonlinelibrary.com) • DOI: 10.1002/cc.452

campuses: college presidents, administrators, policy makers, faculty, university leaders, and administrators, as well as community leaders, activists, and other educational providers. Policy and decision makers at multiple levels may also benefit from this volume through becoming better acquainted with marginalized constituent groups and their needs within their districts. University educators and researchers with an interest in issues involving community colleges and diversity will utilize this volume as another piece of the community college knowledge base and a launching point for subsequent lines of inquiry.

The opening chapter, "Deweyan Democratic Learning Communities and Student Marginalization," by Clifford P. Harbour and Gwyn Ebie, addresses the concept of student marginalization through a framework based on Dewey's 1916 work, *Democracy and Education*. The application of Dewey's framework lays a strong foundation on which to situate the remainder of the volume.

The next two chapters highlight groups of students who are found on many community college campuses. Liza Becker outlines the experiences of Adult English as Second Language learners and how they may be and subsequently feel marginalized during the transition phase in their academic programs. David Horton Jr.'s chapter explores the community college environment through the eyes of student athletes and explains how even though they may seem privileged, athletes, too, may feel marginalized from the rest of the student population.

Eboni M. Zamani-Gallaher and Dibya Devika Choudhuri present a review of available literature that addresses the uniqueness of community college environments and how they are not as inclusive of sexual minorities as one might think. The authors also point out the lack of research on lesbian, gay, bisexual, transgender, and queer (LGBTQ) community college students and provide suggestions for research as well as practical recommendations for those working in the field.

The "Student Veterans and Community Colleges" chapter is very timely in that many community college campuses are experiencing a significant increase in the number of veterans returning from active duty in places such as Afghanistan and Iraq. As these veterans are exchanging their boots for books, the authors shed light on the ways that even these former warriors may feel marginalized and isolated and how community colleges can take steps to develop a more welcoming environment.

In her chapter "Beyond Remedial Dichotomies: Are 'Underprepared' College Students a Marginalized Marjority?," Regina Deil-Amen investigates the way that institutional labeling as either remedial or nonremedial not only marginalizes students but also serves to reinforce an outdated, dichotomous model of remediation. Deil-Amen furthers the argument by positing a broader model that encompasses all underprepared students in community colleges.

Susanna Spaulding studies an often-overlooked community college population in "Working in a Borderland: Stories about Teaching College in

Prison." This chapter invites the reader to consider the experience of being a part-time faculty member who also has to venture into the confines of the correctional facilities. The author addresses the experience of dual marginalization as well as discusses the importance these faculty place on the role they play in their student inmates' lives.

In the final chapter, Susana Hernandez and Ignacio Hernandez present some key resources for anyone who works with or researches marginalized populations. The resources include sources for further reading, existing organizations serving various marginalized groups, and some possible funding opportunities.

As the population of the United States further diversifies, community colleges will continue to be the institution of choice for those looking to find their piece of the American dream. Yet in order to truly be the "people's college," community colleges must continually reexamine their environments to ensure that all who attend are welcomed in to an inclusive environment. It is our hope that this volume can serve as a useful resource in future endeavors for change and support.

Elizabeth M. Cox and Jesse S. Watson
Editors

References

American Association of Community Colleges. Who We Are. Retrieved August 1, 2011, from http://www.aacc.nche.edu/About/Who/Pages/default.aspx.

Cohen, A. M., and Brawer, F. B. *The American Community College* (5th ed.). San Francisco: Jossey-Bass, 2008.

Rhoads, R. A., and Valadez, J. R. *Democracy, Multiculturalism, and the Community College: A Critical Perspective*. New York: Routledge, 1996.

Vigil Laden, B. (ed.). *Serving Minority Populations*. New Directions for Community Colleges, no 127. San Francisco: Jossey-Bass, 2004.

1

Community college faculty and staff committed to the eradication of student marginalization may use a variety of contemporary strategies to address this form of oppression. We seek to complement these strategies by showing how the work of John Dewey may be used to justify the creation and development of democratic learning communities fundamentally opposed to student marginalization.

Deweyan Democratic Learning Communities and Student Marginalization

Clifford P. Harbour, Gwyn Ebie

Community colleges have long been recognized as enrolling a disproportionate share of first-generation college students, low-income students, women, and students of color. Additionally, community colleges have significant enrollments of students who identify as immigrants; lesbian, gay, bisexual, and transgender (LGBT); and disabled. Many of these students have been marginalized in previous educational settings because of their status and identity. Many come to the community college, "democracy's college" (Vaughan, 1985), hoping and expecting to live and study in a more diverse environment free of marginalization. Unfortunately, sometimes these hopes and expectations are not fulfilled and the cycle of marginalization continues.

Other chapters in this volume of *New Directions for Community Colleges* explain why marginalization of community college students occurs and how we can better identify and confront this form of oppression. Most of these works update and extend our understanding of student marginalization by focusing on students' identity and status as the qualities targeted by individual, institutional, and cultural oppression. The purpose of this chapter, however, is to address the subject of student marginalization at the community college from a different perspective. More specifically, the purpose of this work is to outline an ethical framework that could be used to create and justify democratic learning communities fundamentally opposed to student marginalization. This framework is based on core values

New Directions for Community Colleges, no. 155, Fall 2011 © 2011 Wiley Periodicals, Inc.
Published online in Wiley Online Library (wileyonlinelibrary.com) • DOI: 10.1002/cc.453

articulated by John Dewey in his 1916 book *Democracy and Education*. Community colleges have a traditional commitment to priorities generally aligned with some of Dewey's core values (e.g., educational opportunity, individual growth, the importance of the community, and the synthesis of academic and vocational education). Accordingly, we see a discussion of Dewey's work in this context as one that may present valuable insights to community college practitioners and researchers.

However, a few points of clarification are needed. First, we do not offer a philosophical analysis or a critical review of Dewey's work on democracy and education. For more complete interpretations of Dewey's work on these topics we refer readers to excellent publications by Fesmire (2003), Green (1999), Pappas (2008), and Westbrook (1991). Second, our discussion of a Deweyan democratic learning community is limited to our reading of *Democracy and Education*, a text readily available and written for teachers. We acknowledge that a reading of other Dewey publications might lead to a slightly different account of his positions. Third, Dewey's primary objective in writing *Democracy and Education* was to provide public school teachers with a resource to inform their work. Yet Dewey seldom drew stark distinctions, when discussing education and democracy, based on the age of the learner. We choose to follow those who have also relied on *Democracy and Education* as a text with great meaning for education in the broadest sense (e.g., Fesmire, 2003; Green, 1999; Pappas, 2008). We read Dewey's *Democracy and Education* as relevant to community college education except when precluded by the clear meaning of his words. Finally, the core values of a Deweyan democratic learning community do not provide us with the instructional tools needed to construct new teaching strategies, learning assessments, or curricula capable of disassembling student marginalization. What these core values do provide is a practical ethical framework to understand student marginalization as a form of oppression that contradicts the core values of a particular kind of democratic learning community. Our belief is that experienced instructors and students informed by the critical features of a Deweyan democratic learning community are the people best suited to develop the kinds of strategies, assessments, and curricula needed to understand and then resist student marginalization.

In order to accomplish our objective, we have organized our discussion in the following manner. First, we turn to Hardiman and Jackson (1997) for a theory of marginalization, informed by the authors' educational practice, that encompasses individual, institutional, and societal oppression based on status (e.g., low-income, first-generation college student) or identity (e.g., gender, age, race, ethnicity, sexual orientation, disability). Second, we turn to John Dewey's *Democracy and Education* (2008) to explicate specific aspects of his work on education, democracy, and the relationship between education and democracy. In this discussion, we develop a practical ethical framework for constructing democratic learning communities. Finally, with insights gleaned from this discussion, we offer recommendations to institutionalize more democratic learning communities at the community college. We hope our discussion encourages others to revisit Dewey's work and consider how it may be used to confront student marginalization and strengthen what we believe to be the most democratic of postsecondary education institutions, the American community college.

Student Marginalization

We follow Hardiman and Jackson (1997) and define students as marginalized when they are subordinated, discounted, or ignored because of their status or identity as a result of individual behaviors, institutional policies and practices, and social beliefs and conditions that they cannot control. Marginalization is a form of oppression, and at the community college, students may be marginalized in many different ways. Students may be marginalized because of their identity or status by the conscious or unconscious behavior of individuals. An example of this might be when the culturally significant experiences of a Latina student are discounted by an instructor because of his racial and ethnic prejudices. Students may also be marginalized as a result of institutional policies or practices that intentionally or unintentionally subordinate students because of their status or identity. An example of this might be when a college chooses to place noncredit, short-term, service training programs, such as banquet server preparation, in Latino or African American communities but not in White communities. Finally, students may be marginalized as a result of social or cultural beliefs and practices held by members of the dominant community. An example of this might be when a city or town, acting because of unconscious racial prejudice, decides to subsidize transportation services for persons living in dominant culture communities so they can easily attend the community college, while not subsidizing similar transportation services for persons living in minority culture communities. These different scenarios show how student marginalization might be embedded in a variety of individual behaviors, institutional policies, and social or cultural practices that attack students on a very personal level. Often, student marginalization occurs at times when / where and places students are most vulnerable, that is, when they are seeking help and guidance from others.

Our discussion here is not offered as a comprehensive explanation of student marginalization at community colleges. We acknowledge that with the addition of certain assumptions our examples may not demonstrate marginalization. We do not suggest that Hardiman and Jackson's (1997) account of student marginalization is the last word on the subject. However, our examples show that marginalization may be the consequence of conscious or unconscious individual behavior or the result of policies, practices, and beliefs operating at institutions or in the larger society. What places these examples in the same category is that students are subordinated and ignored because of their status or identity, and this impedes their ability to complete their education because of psychological harm (e.g., Schlossberg, 1989) or because of their inability to fight this oppression while facing already daunting work, family, and school responsibilities (Grubb & Lazerson, 2004).

John Dewey and *Democracy* and *Education*

John Dewey (1859–1952) lived before the development of community colleges, and he had very little to say about junior colleges. Dewey's remarks on the education of adults are scattered over a range of writings and do not constitute a complete or systematic account of the topic. An electronic search of Dewey's collected works and correspondence confirms he never used the word *marginalization* or *marginalized* in any of his writings. Given this finding, it is easy to assume that Dewey may offer us little to better understand or confront student marginalization at the community college.

However, in the early decades of the 20th century, Dewey had a great deal to say about education, democracy, and, most important for our purposes, the relationship between education and democracy. After Dewey died, he fell out of favor in the academy and was not read widely in graduate programs in adult education or higher education. Some have suggested this was due to his open support of labor unions, minority groups, and socialist political candidates (Ryan, 1995; Westbrook, 1991). But, whatever the cause of this treatment, Richard Rorty (1978) brought Dewey back to center stage in the academy, and over the past 30 years Dewey's writings have become more widely read in the humanities, social sciences, and the various fields of education. Leading scholars across a range of academic disciplines now identify Dewey as a major 20th-century figure whose writings on education and democracy are especially relevant to early 21st-century America (e.g., Boisvert, 1998; Fesmire, 2003; Green, 1999; Jay, 2002; Pappas, 2008; Rogers, 2009; Ryan, 1995; Westbrook, 1991).

Dewey identified his 1916 book *Democracy and Education* as the text that came closest to providing a complete account of his philosophy (Ryan, 1995). He wrote in his preface that the purpose of the text was to "state the ideas implied in a democratic society and to apply these ideas to the problems of the enterprise of education" (Dewey, 2008, p. 3). His central objective, therefore, was to describe and explain a democracy and then show what its development into a thriving society would require from educational institutions. Dewey characterized a democracy as a way of life that encompassed much more than a democratic government or a democratic process for political decision making. Instead, for him, a democracy was "primarily a mode of associated living, of conjoint communicated experience" (2008, p. 93). Dewey contended that when a democracy was failing, its people were isolated and antisocial. Nations suffering from internal isolation and antisocial beliefs were characterized by (a) families "which seclude their domestic concerns as if they had no connection with a larger life"; (b) schools "separated from the interest of home and community"; and (c) divisions between "rich and poor, learned and unlearned" (p. 91). When a democracy was thriving, however, people had "more numerous and more varied points of shared common interest," and social life was distinguished by "freer interaction between social groups" (p. 92). This freer interaction and communication contributed to "the breaking down of those barriers of class, race, and national identity which kept men from perceiving the full import of their activity" (p. 93). Given the foregoing, we view this free and shared associated living as an essential quality of a Deweyan or thriving democracy and, by extension, as an essential quality of a Deweyan democratic learning community.

Dewey also believed that a thriving democracy was distinguished by its facilitation of individual growth in settings where interaction and communication illuminated common interests. When Dewey discussed individual growth, he included the development of the learner's mind, the acquisition of skills appropriate to an occupation, and the development of democratic character. Growth in these areas was best acquired in a community through shared inquiry. Accordingly, he argued, students should participate in "a large variety of shared undertakings and experiences" to facilitate this kind of development (Dewey, 2008, p. 90). Without shared inquiry, individual growth could lead to a form of individualism characterized by "aloofness and indifference," the "illusion of being really able to stand and act alone," and a blind ignorance of the interrelated nature of modern life (p. 49). A society that promoted this kind of individual growth was inclined to "educate some into masters, . . . educate others into slaves . . . [and] the experience of each party loses in meaning, . . . [because] the free interchange of varying modes of life-experience is arrested" (p. 90). When shared inquiry was present, however, learners could focus on their individual aims while also understanding how they were relevant to the needs and perspectives of others. Therefore, for Dewey (2008), a thriving democracy was distinguished by the maintenance of educational systems that created opportunities for communication of "shared undertakings and experiences" facilitating individual growth (p. 90). In our view, Deweyan democratic learning communities require the same kind of opportunities, shared inquiry, and individual growth.

Dewey (2008) also observed that growth was contingent on an individual's experience and that education throughout human life was "a constant reorganizing or reconstructing of experience" (p. 82). Of course, children and adults have different experiences and therefore grow in different ways. However, in matters of education, he declined to articulate a unique adult perspective, adult need, or adult learning style. Instead, the most significant differences between children and adults concerned the child's lack of experience and the absence of understanding that followed from this and the adult's misunderstanding of experience and the resulting inclination to fall into intellectual ruts and not question beliefs acquired over time. Accordingly, Dewey (2008) stated, "with respect to the development of powers devoted to coping with specific scientific and economic problems we may say the child should be growing in manhood" (p. 55). And, he added, "with respect to sympathetic curiosity, unbiased responsiveness, and openness of mind, we may say that the adult should be growing in childlikeness" (Dewey, 2008, p. 55). For Deweyan democratic learning communities serving adult learners, therefore, one of the greatest challenges is to overcome intellectual ruts and prejudice and instead facilitate communication, interaction, and learning in an open and unbiased manner.

As we noted earlier, Dewey believed that education in a thriving democracy should promote individual growth as a consequence of shared inquiry. But this did not mean educational aims or purposes should be determined by some external authority such as the government or industry. Instead, Dewey (2008) explained that appropriate educational aims should have three qualities. They should be based on the learner's experience and develop as "an outgrowth of existing conditions" (p. 111). They should be flexible and "capable of alteration to meet circumstances" (p. 111). And they should guide the learner through the activity of learning and not identify a specific end or conclusion. Considered collectively, Dewey claimed that educational aims should be flexible guides that promote continuing growth based on the individual's experience. Along with our preceding conclusions, we read Dewey as stating that this quality would also be a core value for democratic learning communities in a thriving democracy.

Dewey acknowledged that individual growth occurs in many different settings. But in public institutional settings, he was a strong advocate for occupational education. He used the term *occupation* to refer to a student's continuing involvement in social enterprises that could be pursued over the course of a lifetime (e.g., gardening, construction, or food preparation). Dewey understood education in an occupation as a much broader activity than what we typically associate with vocational instruction today. Accordingly, Dewey (2008) argued that:

> an education which acknowledges the full intellectual and social meaning of a vocation would include instruction in the historic background of present conditions; training in science to give intelligence and initiative in dealing with material and agencies of production; and study of economics, civics and politics, to bring the future worker into touch with the problems of the day and the various methods proposed for its improvement. (p. 328)

Dewey rejected the traditional distinction between vocational and liberal education and criticized educational systems providing a "traditional liberal or cultural education for the few economically able to enjoy it" while assigning to "the masses a narrow technical trade education for specialized callings, carried on under the control of others" (Dewey, 2008, p. 329).

Moreover, Dewey argued that when a person's education was focused on an occupation, several specific advantages followed. First, an occupation "balances the distinctive capacity of an individual with his social service. To find out what one is fitted to do and to secure an opportunity to do it is the key to happiness" (Dewey, 2008, p. 318). No other form of education had this positive consequence. Second, "education *through* occupations . . . combines within itself more of the factors conducive to learning than any other method" (p. 319). An education focused on an occupation was an education with a purpose and an education that incorporated several different kinds of learning. Third, Dewey believed that adequate training for an occupation must include the communication, learning, and work a person did while actively engaged in the practice of that occupation as it existed in the real world. Finally, Dewey firmly rejected the notion that students could select an occupation in their youth and then settle into it for the balance of their lives. He stated, "it is a conventional and arbitrary view which assumes that discovery of the work to be chosen for adult life is made once for all at some particular date" (p. 321). And, he added, occupational education should provide students with a "power of readaptation" so they do not become "blindly subject to a fate imposed upon them" by economic forces (Dewey, 2008, p. 328). For Dewey, practical holistic education for life must be centered on an occupation, and we read this as another core value of democratic learning communities in a thriving democracy.

Finally, Dewey argued that education also provided an important means of social transformation. On this point, Dewey (2008) stated, "A curriculum which acknowledges the social responsibilities of education must present situations where problems are relevant to the problems of living together, and where observation and information are calculated to develop social insight and interest" (p. 200). Social transformation required more, however, than an affirmative focus on the challenges of living together. Public educational institutions also needed to prevent the undue influence of private economic interests. Accordingly, Dewey (2008) said, "democracy cannot flourish where the chief influences in selecting subject matter of instruction are utilitarian ends narrowly conceived for the masses, and, for the higher education of the few, the traditions of a specialized cultivated class" (p. 200). Instead, he argued, education must provide learners with opportunities to see past the limitations of contemporary society and envision a better world in the future.

It is critical to note that Dewey was not the naïve utopian he is sometimes made out to be. He did not believe education could alone transform the society. Social transformation also required changes in governmental policies and social and economic structures to provide people with more control over their work and their lives. But, in concert with social and economic reorganization and revision in government policies, education offered an essential and constructive vehicle for social transformation. This transformation depended, at least in part, on educational experiences in which learners examined the challenges of living together in order to develop shared interests and insights into what a better future might look like. We read this priority as another core value of a democratic learning community.

Our discussion above has reviewed critical passages from Dewey's *Democracy and Education* to show how this work outlines the core values and qualities that we see as essential to a democratic learning community. This community is characterized by its commitments to (a) free and shared associated living, (b) individual growth through communication and shared undertakings and experiences, (c) open and unbiased learning, (d) learning guided by the flexible and experientially based needs of the learner, (e) practical holistic education for life, and (f) education focused on greater social awareness and shared interests. These six qualities reveal a consistent emphasis on the development of the individual learner based on her unique identity and experiences in the context of a community committed to communication, shared living, shared undertakings, and shared interests. We read Dewey's consistent emphasis on individual growth as signaling an uncompromising commitment to the development of learners in ways important to them based on their identity and experiences. And this individual growth must not simply be accepted or tolerated within the community but shared in the full or vital sense of the term. For Dewey, the shared living, shared undertakings, and shared interests that distinguish a thriving democracy are the result of the kind of conscious communication and interaction that effect deep change in how individuals think and act. As he stated in the opening pages of *Democracy and Education*, "communication is a process of sharing experience till it becomes a common possession. It modifies the disposition of both the parties who partake in it" (Dewey, 2008, p. 12).

We contend that Deweyan learning communities found in a thriving democracy would be well prepared to identify and confront student marginalization. These communities would practice the kind of communication and sharing that has the power to illuminate the behaviors, policies, and beliefs that marginalize individuals. They would practice the kind of close communication and experiential learning that promotes individual growth. Finally, Dewey's emphasis on shared living, shared undertakings, and shared interests indicates that these democratic learning communities would share a commitment to inclusion in life, in work, and in identifying the duties and rights of all members of the community.

To be sure, there is nothing magical about a Deweyan democratic learning community. The mere articulation of an ethical framework has never automatically changed the beliefs and behaviors of community members. And we recognize the creation of a democratic learning community based on these core values would not immediately dissolve significant power imbalances that inhibit the ability of instructors, staff, and administrators to take concrete steps to limit student marginalization. The power of the dominant culture would continue to flow through individuals, institutions, and social structures in conscious and unconscious ways that reinforce marginalization.

However, Dewey's discussion in *Democracy and Education* can serve as an ethical justification for developing the kind of democratic learning communities capable of validating individual identities and experiences and confronting student marginalization in a way that helps form stronger democratic learning communities characterized by deeper and more extensive relationships between members. So these communities would give us a new language and new ethical framework to work toward the end of marginalization based on a student's identity or status. Perhaps most importantly, a new narrative could explain how the marginalization of students not only oppresses them and undermines their success but poses a great impediment to the development of our democracy.

Recommendations

Establishment of democratic learning communities based on Deweyan core values would require substantial time and effort. We offer the following recommendations to start this communication or build on already existing initiatives consistent with Dewey's *Democracy and Education*. This dialogue could begin within existing faculty groups and student organizations:

1. Identify specific examples of student marginalization on campus and explain how they are inconsistent with the core values of a Deweyan democratic learning community.
2. Explain what kind of Deweyan dialogue and action is most likely to succeed in eradicating student marginalization.
3. Generate greater awareness of the concept "thriving democracy" and identify the gaps between existing learning communities (perhaps in specific courses or programs) and Deweyan democratic learning communities.
4. Celebrate John Dewey's birthday and offer historical and biographical presentations showing how he worked to identify and confront various forms of oppression.
5. Establish a reading group to study Dewey's *Democracy and Education* and identify other aspects of the text that are relevant to student marginalization.

Conclusion

Because student marginalization may be manifested in individual actions, institutional policies, and social practices, it is a pernicious problem that can arise at many different times and at many different places. When students must confront marginalization at the same time that they are seeking to develop themselves, Dewey's work provides an ethical framework that can support community college students, faculty, staff, and administrators as they work together to develop their democratic learning communities. Dewey's writings offer us the hope and the vision to regroup and move forward together on the road to a deeper democracy.

References

Boisvert, R. D. *John Dewey: Rethinking our time*. Albany, NY: State University of New York Press, 1998.

Dewey, J. Democracy and education. In J. A. Boydston (ed.), *The middle works 1899–1924: John Dewey, Volume 9, Democracy and education 1916* (pp. 3–402). Carbondale, IL: Southern Illinois University Press, 2008.

Fesmire, S. *John Dewey and moral imagination: Pragmatism in ethics*. Indianapolis: Indiana University Press, 2003.

Green, J. M. *Deep democracy: Community, diversity and transformation*. Lanham, MD: Rowman & Littlefield, 1999.

Grubb, W. N., & Lazerson, M. *The education gospel: The economic power of schooling*. Cambridge, MA: Harvard University Press, 2004.

Hardiman, R., & Jackson, B. W. Conceptual foundations for social justice courses. In M. Adams, L. A. Bell, & P. Griffin (eds), *Teaching for diversity and social justice* (pp. 16–29). New York, NY: Routledge, 1997.

Jay, M. *The education of John Dewey: A biography*. New York, NY: Columbia University Press, 2002.

Pappas, G. *John Dewey's ethics: Democracy as experience*. Indianapolis: Indiana University Press, 2008.

Rogers, M. L. *The undiscovered Dewey: Religion, morality, and the ethos of democracy*. New York, NY: Columbia University Press, 2009.

Rorty, R. *Philosophy and the mirror of nature*. Princeton, NJ: Princeton University Press, 1978.

Ryan, A. *John Dewey and the high tide of American Liberalism*. New York, NY: Norton, 1995.

Schlossberg, N. K. Marginality and mattering: Key issues in building community. In D. C. Roberts (ed.), Designing campus activities to foster a sense of community. *New Directions for Student Services*, No. 48. (pp. 5–15). San Francisco, CA: Jossey-Bass, 1989.

Vaughan, G. B. Maintaining open access and comprehensiveness. In D. Puyear (ed.), Maintaining institutional integrity. *New Directions for Community Colleges*, no. 52 (pp. 17–28). San Francisco, CA: Jossey-Bass, 1985.

Westbrook, R. B. *John Dewey and American democracy*. Ithaca, NY: Cornell University Press, 1991.

CLIFFORD P. HARBOUR *is an associate professor in the adult and postsecondary education program at the University of Wyoming.*

GWYN EBIE *is a professor of business and technology and a discipline coordinator for technology at Colorado Mountain College's Aspen Campus.*

2

This chapter raises awareness of the role that educational and socioeconomic background plays in the perceived sense of marginality and the decision-making process for adult immigrant learners who are preparing to transition from the highest levels of noncredit ESL to credit programs and postsecondary degree pathways.

Noncredit to Credit Transitioning Matters for Adult ESL Learners in a California Community College

Liza A. Becker

> You know, for me it's just a good gift—a surprise gift for me to continue to school. Maybe right now I have a chance to go to university. I . . . maybe, I could improve myself. If the chance coming, I could find better job. I always dream I could melt in the American life, like other people, and just like don't think I'm foreigner, just totally different.
>
> Lei, age 43, engineer from China

Throughout our nation's history, immigrants have come to the United States seeking opportunities for socioeconomic mobility, to strengthen family ties, or secure personal freedom. To leave the familiar landscape is not a decision made lightly and, once having resettled in their new home, immigrants face choices that may relegate them to the margins or pull them closer toward advancement opportunities. Effective use of English, the dominant language, becomes a vital skill in helping them to gain the cultural and social connectedness necessary for a successful transition (Bourdieu, 1982/1991). Many of these adult immigrants turn to tuition-free, noncredit English as a Second Language (ESL) programs to gain communicative fluency as well as an entry point to credit and postsecondary degree pathways. For some English learners, making this academic transition from noncredit to credit facilitates a successful transition to their new

NEW DIRECTIONS FOR COMMUNITY COLLEGES, no. 155, Fall 2011 © 2011 Wiley Periodicals, Inc.
Published online in Wiley Online Library (wileyonlinelibrary.com) • DOI: 10.1002/cc.454

life; for others, the noncredit-to-credit experience is an arduous journey with many obstacles along the way.

This chapter draws from a study that explored issues of transitioning from noncredit ESL to credit programs for *adult immigrants* at a large suburban community college located in southern California. Adult learners are nontraditional students who have external obligations and demands that complicate and often conflict with their academic pursuits (Brookfield, 1986; Giancola, Grawitch, and Borchert, 2009). The participants were enrolled in a two-semester ESL Bridge program at Sunkist Community College (program, college, and participant names are pseudonyms) offered through the continuing education division. They had completed the highest level of noncredit ESL and were at an academic crossroads in terms of their next steps and future educational plans. Through semistructured interviews, 17 participants with varying socioeconomic, educational, and ethnic backgrounds shared their experiences and aspirations for social mobility in their adopted homeland. At the time of the interviews, nine of the ESL Bridge participants had successfully completed at least one credit course, six participants had postponed their transitioning plans, and two participants declared no intention of enrolling in credit classes in the near future.

The information provided by the learners was interpreted through Bourdieu's constructs of *cultural capital*, the exposure to and level of educational and socioeconomic backgrounds of the learners, and *habitus*, the socially conditioned behaviors and perceptions that tacitly affect students' decision-making processes and their academic mobility (Bourdieu, 1972/1977). Narratives of the participants were coded and analyzed using a phenomenological design (Moustakas, 1994) that highlights the common experiences shared by the individuals. Themes emerged that were aligned with level of educational background and socioeconomic status of the ESL learners in their native countries.

Complex factors are involved in the academic journey of adult immigrant learners who desire to integrate into the scholastic and postsecondary educational arenas of the community college and beyond. Prominent among the major findings were the facilitative role of noncredit ESL instruction and student support for *all* the noncredit ESL learners. Individuals who immigrated with the right resources such as a strong educational background and well-established careers (i.e., high cultural capital) used the noncredit ESL program as leverage to social mobility and to help them reclaim a more centralized role in their new homeland. Conversely, immigrants who were marginalized in their countries of origin and driven to seek social and economic mobility in the United States had difficulty continuing along a desired academic pathway into credit. Although they had gained self-confidence and cultural capital in the workplace—particularly in comparison with coworkers who had not invested time in learning English—participants with low cultural capital still expressed a sense of marginality within the academic setting.

NEW DIRECTIONS FOR COMMUNITY COLLEGES • DOI: 10.1002/cc

The Issue in Context

The shifting demographic profile of California is becoming more evident with each decade of census reporting. According to the Public Policy Institute of California, the state often serves as a "crucible for immigrant-related issues in the United States . . . due to the overwhelming share of U.S. immigrants who choose to live in the state" (Bohn, 2009, p. 4). According to the 2000 U.S. Census Report, the population of immigrants in the state climbed from 9 percent in 1970 to 26 percent in 2000; projections of data yet to be released indicate an upward trajectory of 28 percent to 30 percent between the years 2010 and 2025. The benefits gained by a college education and a postsecondary degree are well recognized by these new-comers and well documented by researchers as a means to improve quality of life and promote the health and welfare of society at large (Grubb, Badway, and Bell, 2003; McMahon, 2009). Unfortunately, there is also emerging evidence of an immense gap in what immigrant learners intend to achieve and actual attainment of their academic and career goals (Moore & Shulock, 2009; Van Noy, Jacobs, Korey, Bailey, and Hughes, 2008). Recent noncredit accountability reports show that a relatively low percentage of noncredit students are transitioning to credit within the community college system; however, those who do transition are indicating a high success rate of completion in subsequent terms. In other words, few are able to pro-gress, but those who do are well on their way to a postsecondary degree (California Community Colleges System Office, 2008). Although such data is informative, it is difficult to interpret and apply toward program improve-ment without a more comprehensive grasp of the complex factors involved in defining success for adult immigrant learners. One thing cannot be dis-puted: immigrants from all backgrounds and levels of cultural capital are drawn to noncredit ESL programs with high hopes of a brighter future and the attainment of the American dream.

Marginality and Mattering for Adult Immigrant Learners.   Often, community college practitioners view ESL learners as a homogenous group with limited English proficiency. Such broad impressions generally fail to account for the large array of backgrounds and needs the immigrant learners bring with them to the educational environment (Blumenthal, 2002; Szelényi and Chang, 2002). In the beginning, all immigrants have the shared experi-ence that they are outsiders looking in. Some will negotiate their way from the margins of their new social setting toward the center by utilizing their preexisting knowledge and cultural capital as resources (Bourdieu & Passeron, 1977/1990). Others, unfortunately, will remain on the border as observers rather than active participants. This sense of *marginality*, accord-ing to Schlossberg (1989), is the perception of detachment from the domi-nant culture; it not only provokes anxiety but also negatively affects the stamina and motivation necessary to reach a desired goal. The sense of *mat-tering*, however, allows one to feel connected and valued as a member of a particular community or institution (Schlossberg, 1989). Factors that affect the learners' sense of connectedness to the institution include the physical proximity of their classes to the "heart" of the campus, the acknowledgment and appreciation of diverse learning styles by instructors, and the inclusion of nontraditional students in college mission of access and success (O'Donnell and Tobbell, 2007; Schlossberg, 1989; Valadez, 1993). Yet, even in the most robust noncredit programs within California's community college system, evidence suggests that *equitable access* to noncredit instruction and support services do not guarantee *equal success* for all learners (California Community Colleges System Office, 2008). A growing body of literature is turning to Pierre Bourdieu's constructs of cultural capital and habitus as a lens through which we can better understand the issues of student success for underrepresented populations of learners.

The Role of Cultural Capital and Habitus in Academic Progress. Even under the most auspicious circumstances, adult immigrant learners enrolled in the community college find themselves in a new cultural environment grappling with issues that include English language proficiency, gaining financial security, navigating a foreign educational system, and redefining their self-identity. How they manage such personal issues while studying can significantly affect their academic progress and desire for degree attainment. Bourdieu's (1972/1977) constructs of cultural capital and habitus overlay the experiences of immigrant learners in the educational setting with ease. Immigrants are literally and figuratively in transition from one cultural landscape to another. From the margins of a new homeland, they are negotiating their prospects for acculturation and long-term success. *Cultural capital* in the educational context is the accumulation of scholastic wealth such as transitioning to credit programs that lead to a postsecondary degree; such actions help the individual to gain symbolic power of a degree—an emblem of achievement that is valued by our society—and to advance toward a more centralized position in the educational field of action. *Habitus* is defined as the conscious and unconscious actions and perceptions of learners that impact academic and social mobility (Bourdieu, 1972/1977). Through our habitus, all of us react to situations in ways that reflect generational conditioning; this becomes a critical factor for learners who are first-generation college attendees—as is the case with the majority of noncredit ESL learners.

The academic progress of adult immigrant learners enrolled in noncredit ESL programs is visually represented in Figure 2.1 through the Bourdieusian lens of an individual's cultural capital background and actions of habitus. The journey itself is symbolized in the form of an arrow that stops and starts to accommodate the demands and challenges faced by immigrants when they first enroll in noncredit classes. Learners, particularly those with lower cultural capital (e.g., at or below a high school education, or marginalized status even in their native country) begin their journey with limited access to resources and, with time and educational capital, gain

Figure 2.1. Academic Progress of Adult Immigrant Learners from Noncredit ESL to Credit Programs

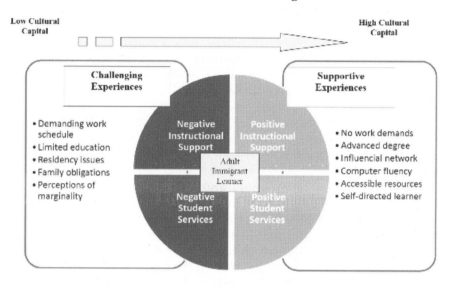

mobility and advancement toward a more secure future. Supportive and impeding factors exist both within the educational program and in their personal lives. At the institutional level, student support services and a robust curriculum that meets their needs will help them to advance, while lack of resources or their inability to access existing resources will impede their progress. Outside of the classroom, students express a variety of support systems that facilitate their progress or that interfere with their plans to progress from noncredit to credit programs in the community college. At the heart of the figure are the adult immigrant learners who continuously experience, evaluate, and utilize resources available to them. A critical component of this model is the dynamics between learners, the accessibility of resources, and their ability to maximize use of the available resources. As educators, our goal is to facilitate the academic success of our learners, and to do so we need a deeper understanding of their experiences.

The Sunkist Study

Sunkist Community College was an ideal site to study the perceptions and decisions of advanced learners who are exiting the highest levels of the noncredit ESL program. An overwhelming majority of the noncredit ESL learners are adults (85 percent over 23 years of age), and they select college or job/career advancement as a primary goal for their English improvement upon program entry, mirroring other noncredit programs within the system. Its comprehensive instructional and student support services provided a rich backdrop to investigate the issues and concerns of adult immigrants within the college system. To make the transition as seamless as possible, Sunkist's noncredit ESL program housed in the continuing education division has established a direct articulation agreement with the credit ESL program within the humanities division; this allows advanced noncredit learners to enroll in credit ESL and other courses without having to reapply or take another placement test within the same institution. Another strong feature of the program is the structure of the noncredit ESL Bridge program. The two-semester program is offered as a cohort model with an integrated curriculum in courses such as Advanced ESL Speaking, Advanced ESL Writing, Career and Life Planning (taught by ESL counselors), Keyboarding, Microcomputer Applications, English (credit ESL is promoted though not mandated), and a credit or noncredit elective in their field of interest. With these strong teaching and counseling components embedded within the program, approximately 27 percent of the ESL Bridge students transitioned successfully into credit by completing at least one credit course—more than double the reported average for the state (California Community Colleges System Office, 2008). The long-standing mission that guides the program, however, is to increase access, persistence, and success for those who are most in need of socioeconomic mobility. By interviewing a cross-section of ESL Bridge students, patterns of experiences emerged that help us to understand the complex factors influencing academic progress of adult immigrants who study in our noncredit ESL programs. In the following section I share the results of 17 interviews with advanced ESL learners who completed the ESL Bridge program and either continued on the credit pathway or postponed the transition due to one or more impediments.

Learners with High Cultural Capital.   The cohort that successfully transitioned to credit shared common characteristics that included a predisposition of privilege (Bourdieu and Passeron, 1977/1990) from their countries of origin, providing them with higher cultural capital in the United States than their counterparts. They came to the United States with advanced degrees, active social lives, leisurely travels, and strong financial stability. Their countries of origin included China, Colombia, El Salvador, Korea, Kuwait, Mexico, Peru, and Vietnam. Most of them had well-established professional careers—architect, nurse, engineer, university lecturer, special education teacher, and school proprietor—that were left behind in order to be closer to family or to escape from oppressive regimes. Most of this transitioning cohort elected not to work in the United States or managed to control their work hours through volunteerism or as independent consultants. Important to note is their shared sense of familiarity and comfort within the academic environment. According to Bourdieu (1972/1977), individual members of a class that have high cultural capital know how to access resources within the system through their habitus; this allows them to maintain their current status or to gain mobility. In essence, these immigrant learners had strong educational backgrounds and experiences in their native countries, which provided them with the knowledge, comfort, and means by which to pursue their educational plans of a new postsecondary degree. As adults, they had a strong sense of identity that was formed long before they came to the United States (Brookfield, 1986). Ironically, it was the awareness of their shift in self-identity and sense of marginality in a new culture that propelled the members of this group to seek the community college path as a means toward readjusting and trying to regain the centralized class and position they left behind. Consequently, one of the primary experiences they shared was their internal struggle to recalibrate and settle into life in the United States. Their biggest challenge was their shifting sense of who they were, where they fit in their new cultural milieu, and with which social groups to associate—and from which groups to distance themselves.

Learners with Low Cultural Capital.   The majority of interviewees with low cultural capital had to postpone their enrollment into credit courses due to intervening life circumstances. Their intentions, however, were to resolve their personal issues and to take credit courses at some point within the next academic year. All of the participants came from low socioeconomic backgrounds and shared personal histories of financial hardship and poor working conditions—all were from Mexico. Only one of the participants had completed a technical college (secretarial and fashion design); the educational range of the remaining cohort ranged from second grade through high school. Although their experiences were similar to others in their local towns and smaller communities, they still presented a sense of marginalization from the dominant class in Mexico. Bourdieu (1993) defines this reproduction of marginality for the participants with low cultural capital as the tacit and generational social conditioning that is their habitus. Their perceived position within the dominant culture as well as in the academic arena is explained by Bourdieu and Passeron as the result of a "process of inculcation" that produces primarily unconscious behaviors and "internalized principles . . . durable and transposable" over time and space (1977/1990, pp. 31–34). Though afforded seemingly equal opportunities through the noncredit ESL program, these participants alluded to inherent personal and language-group deficiencies in the academic arena as reasons for postponing their transition into credit. This cohort often referenced themselves as "wasting time in class" or referred to classmates from other countries as "smart" in comparison to themselves. Unlike their counterparts with high cultural capital, maintaining stability in wage earnings took priority over school when they experienced conflict in terms of time and energy. According to Giancola et al. (2009), the educational environment was an area over which the adult learners in college had the least amount of control. All but one of the participants in this cohort had full-time jobs; the one participant who did not work elected to stay home as a full-time mom (her husband was unemployed). Despite the hardships of time and finance, this cohort indicated that they had made significant advances, considering their starting point in terms of socioeconomic mobility; all were proud of their relative great gains in comparison to their former cultural status in Mexico. Additionally, many of the participants in this cohort stated that when they entered the noncredit ESL program, their only intention was to improve their English in order to better communicate in the workplace. Over time, the noncredit ESL experience in general, and the ESL Bridge program in particular, provided them with new options for their future academic and career plans.

Breaking through the Barrier.   Bourdieu stated that habitus was not static and predetermined; individuals with opportunity, information, and access can consciously or unconsciously break from their generational history and forge a new path (Wacquant, 1989). Several participants in the Sunkist study seemed to fit in the "low cultural capital" cohort, yet had made a successful transition into credit. A prime example of a participant who utilized such interaction-based strategies was Tran, who was driven to attain a vocational degree from Sunkist College. Tran had no education beyond high school and shared more in common with the participants from the postponing group. Nevertheless, he was successfully completing his credit courses and well on his way toward earning his vocational certificate in interior design. How Tran differed from some of the other participants with no experience beyond high school seemed to be in his utilization of counseling services. He was proactive in making personal appointments with ESL counselors in order to access important information (e.g., financial aid); this form of agency was commonly represented by the learners with high cultural capital. Receiving financial support for his credit tuition allowed Tran to tend to his studies with focus and determination. Despite his self-acknowledged difficulties to communicate effectively with native-English speakers, Tran persisted with his credit studies and was nevertheless able to maintain steady progress.

Another example of a participant with drive and resilience was Reina, the only participant in the transitioned group to balance a full-time job with full-time studies and other demands. Despite her incredibly difficult time with multiple roles as an adult learner, Reina was successfully working toward completing her associate's degree and transferring to a local university. According to Morales (2008), academic resiliency refers to "educational achievement outcome anomalies that occur after an individual has been exposed to statistical risk factors" (2008, p. 228). Reina was able to persist with her academic progress as she maintained high grades for her financial aid, a full-time workload as a store manager, and personal affairs that included an ailing mother. She was reflective during the interview about her academic resiliency and articulated ways in which she dealt with each obstacle that would arise in her life. Regarding her sense of marginalization in credit classes, Reina stated the following:

NEW DIRECTIONS FOR COMMUNITY COLLEGES • DOI: 10.1002/cc

You know when you have [credit] class and the teacher says, "So, make a group with five people." Right now, you know, my accent and my English . . . sometimes, people discriminate, the way you speak. It happened to me. So, I don't worry about that. I don't be afraid of that thing, so I go to group, so I can listen to them and sometimes they don't want to make. . . . This is kind of hard for people from other countries to work with young people in this country. Because, some of them, not always, but some of them are rude with you when don't speak clear and you don't have, probably . . . they think that you are not good for the class, or something like that. But you have to show them that you have, the capacity, you have the skill. Probably, your speaking is not well as them, but you have the power to do it, too, so many things, whatever you want. You have the opportunity to try.

Reina was able to step back and assess challenging situations and to reflect on them as learning experiences. Morales (2008) discovered that learners like Reina who exhibit long-term academic resilience are able to make use of their metacognitive abilities to assess themselves within the social context and to redirect their thoughts and actions in a productive way. According to Bourdieu (as cited in Wacquant, 1989), individuals often make "strategic calculations of costs and benefits which tends to carry out at a conscious level" (p. 45). The examples of Reina and Tran suggest that knowledge acquisition and reflective strategies result in conscious and deliberate action by adult immigrant learners to maximize benefit for themselves and lead to social mobility in the United States.

Implications and Recommendations

A primary mission for noncredit ESL programs within the California community college system is to ease the acculturation and active participation of adult immigrant learners as productive members of their new homeland. One way to achieve this is to facilitate a successful academic and career pathway that leads to a postsecondary degree and higher wage earnings. The participants who were interviewed for the Sunkist Community College study came from a bridge-to-credit program designed to facilitate the transition process of advanced ESL learners. Findings of the study indicate that transitioning to credit requires involvement and commitment from the entire community of practice—learners, instructors, administrators, and staff.

The successful transition for noncredit ESL learners necessitates both an awareness of options and effective communication skills. At the classroom level, providing insightful and relevant ESL curriculum that goes beyond text-based exercises can present opportunities for learners to reflect on their aspirations and plans for attainment. Bourdieu (1972/1977) stated that habitus may be deeply ingrained yet can be uncovered and reflected upon by the individual. In line with this is Norton's (1997) emancipatory stance regarding language learning and identity, stating that communicative competence should include the right to speak and to be heard. Integrating themes that deal with identity and marginality/mattering, for example, can be thought provoking and emancipatory—so long as the lessons are presented within a safe and nurturing classroom environment. Such lessons can also prepare learners to express themselves in order to be understood by native English speakers—faculty, younger students, and college staff—with whom they will be in contact on a regular basis.

At the program levels of an institution, developing integration services will greatly enhance the successful transition for noncredit ESL learners who are contemplating degree pathways. The noncredit ESL program at Sunkist College made sure that new and continuing learners had multiple venues and means of accessing information regarding the educational system in the United States. Their ubiquitous services reached the learners through orientations, classroom presentations, student newsletters, career conferences, and, for the most advanced-level learners, a designated course in career and educational planning. The value of such accessibility became evident in the interviews. For example, two of the most frequently mentioned elements of program support mentioned by the ESL Bridge participants were the Career and Life Planning course and the ESL counselors who taught them. The integration of instruction and support services may begin with such simple actions as in-class matriculation presentations and guest speakers from credit programs.

At the institutional level, the greater college community needs to engage in dialogue with ESL experts (colleagues from both credit and noncredit programs) regarding the issues and challenges that are inherent in second language acquisition for adult learners. Such dialog can include tolerance of minor language errors that do not interfere with coursework and class performance, supplemental support such as tutoring in the classroom, or developing learning communities or paired courses that continue to provide advanced ESL strategies and techniques within specific content areas. Ideally, an articulation agreement or direct pathway between noncredit and credit ESL accompanied by priority registration status can provide a strong bridge to credit, as was the case with this study site. In summary, effective elements that support the learning progress for noncredit ESL learners should include reflective and emancipatory curriculum, an integrated instructional and support program, and an inclusive dialogue with the community of practice.

Conclusion

California leads the nation as a destination for immigrants entering the United States in search of socioeconomic mobility, with the greatest concentration of new settlements in the Los Angeles and San Francisco regions (Bohn, 2009). Many of these immigrants turn to noncredit ESL programs

NEW DIRECTIONS FOR COMMUNITY COLLEGES • DOI: 10.1002/cc

offered through the community college system; they view language enhancement as the means to academic and vocational advancement in their new homeland. As adults, they understand the value our society places on academic credentials, and those with adequate resources (i.e., high cultural capital and the accompanying habitus) are able to take advantage of the resources and support toward academic advancement. Others with more humble backgrounds and limited resources have aspirations for academic progress and have a longer path to traverse. Community colleges and noncredit programs, in particular, have an important role to play in promoting the advancement of *all* immigrants for the well-being of all humankind. The voices and narratives of adult immigrants are vital to understanding and improving educational and social mobility in the learners' adopted homeland.

References

Blumenthal, A. English as a second language at the community college: An exploration of context and concerns. *New Directions for Community Colleges,* No. 117, San Francisco, CA: Jossey-Bass, 2002.

Bohn, S. *New patterns of immigrant settlement in California,* 2009. Retrieved from the Public Policy Institute of California (PPIC) web site: www.ppic.org/main/publication. asp?i=812.

Bourdieu, P. *Outline of a theory of practice.* New York, NY: Cambridge University Press, 1972/1977.

Bourdieu, P. *Language and symbolic power.* Cambridge, MA: Harvard University Press, 1982/1991.

Bourdieu, P. *The field of cultural production: Essays on art and literature.* New York, NY: Columbia University Press, 1993.

Bourdieu, P., & Passeron, J. *Reproduction in education, society and culture,* 2nd ed. London, UK: Sage, 1977/1990.

Brookfield, S. *Understanding and facilitating adult learning.* San Francisco, CA: Jossey-Bass, 1986.

California Community Colleges System Office. *Career development and college preparation in the state: Supplement to the 2008 ARCC report,* 2008. Retrieved from the California Community Colleges Chancellor's Office web site: www.ccco .eduHYPERLINK"http://www.ccco.edu/"/Portals/4/TRIS/research/reports/cdcp_report _june_08.pdf.

Giancola, J., Grawitch, M., & Borchert, D. Dealing with the stress of college: A model for adult students. *Adult Education Quarterly,* 2009, 59(3), 246–263. DOI: 10.1177/0741713609331479.

Grubb, W., Badway, N., & Bell, D. Community colleges and the equity agenda: The potential for noncredit education. *Annals of the American Academy of Political and Social Sciences,* 2003, 586, 218–240. DOI: 10.1177/0002716202250226.

McMahon, W. *Higher learning, greater good: The private and social benefits of higher education.* Baltimore, MD: Johns Hopkins University Press, 2009.

Moore, C., & Shulock, N. *The grades are in—2008: Is California higher education measuring up?,* 2009. Retrieved from www.csus.edu/ihelp/.

Morales, E. Academic resilience in retrospect: Following up a decade later. *Journal of Hispanic Higher Education,* 2008, 7(228), 228–249. DOI: 10.1177/1538192708317119.

Moustakas, C. *Phenomenological research methods.* Thousand Oaks, CA: Sage, 1994.

Norton, B. Language, identity, and the ownership of English. *TESOL Quarterly,* 1997, *31*(3), 409–429.

O'Donnell, V., & Tobbell, J. The transition of adult education students to higher education: Legitimate peripheral participation in a community of practice? *Adult Education Quarterly,* 2007, *57*(312). DOI: 10.1177/0741713607302686.

Schlossberg, N. Marginality and mattering: Key issues in building community. In D.C. Roberts (ed.), Designing campus activities to foster a sense of community. *New Directions for Student Services,* 1989, No. 48. San Francisco, CA: Jossey-Bass.

Szelényi, K., & Chang, J. Educating immigrants: The community college role. *Community College Review,* 2002, *30*(2), 55–73.

Valadez, J. Cultural capital and its impact on the aspirations of nontraditional community college students. *Community College Review,* 1993, *21*(30), 1–15. DOI: 10.1177/009155219302100304

Van Noy, M., Jacobs, J., Korey, S., Bailey, T., & Hughes, K. *The landscape of noncredit workforce education: State policies and community college practices,* 2008. Retrieved from the New York: Columbia University, Teachers College, Community College Research Center website:www.aacc.nche.edu/Publications/Reports/Pages/default.aspx.

Wacquant, L. Toward a reflexive sociology: A workshop with Pierre Bourdieu. *Sociological Theory,* 1989, *7*(1), 26–63.

LIZA A. BECKER *is director of the English as a Second Language department at Mt. San Antonio College in Walnut, California.*

3

This chapter describes the marginalization of student athletes and provides case studies and recommendations for institutions interested in better supporting, encouraging, and responding to the needs of students within this population.

Developing an Institutional Culture toward Degree Attainment for Student Athletes

David Horton, Jr.

College athletes are often labeled as privileged, lazy, incapable, and disinterested students who are motivated to enroll in higher education only for the sole purpose of participating in athletics (Sailes, 1993; Watson, 2003). These students are also often stigmatized by their faculty, coaches, and nonathlete peers (Simons, Bosworth, Fujita, & Jensen, 2007). Simons and colleagues (2007) identified a stigmatized individual as one who has attributes that are deeply discredited and seen by others as tainted.

Within higher education, the label "student athlete" has been severely discredited and tainted by the actions of a few, relatively speaking, misdirected and misguided coaches and student athletes (Purdy, Eitzen, & Hufnagel, 1982; Sailes, 1993). Their actions have led to the proliferation of negative perceptions which reinforce the dumb jock, low intelligence stereotype. These perceptions, combined with institutions' low expectations for athletes' academic performance and goals, have had a significant impact on students' collegiate experiences, social engagement with nonathlete peers, and ability to be academically successful (Beilock & McConnell, 2004; Harrison, 2008). Inevitably, student athletes begin to accept and own these perceptions as reality, which is a process Steele (1997) termed *stereotype threat*. Specifically, stereotype threat is the process in which an individual lives out negative stereotypes that have been placed on him due to his group membership or how he self-identifies. In turn, institutions use these resulting student behaviors to justify placing even lower expectations

New Directions for Community Colleges, no. 155, Fall 2011 © 2011 Wiley Periodicals, Inc.
Published online in Wiley Online Library (wileyonlinelibrary.com) • DOI: 10.1002/cc.455

on athletes' behavior, both in and out of the classroom; thus, the cycle leading to marginalization of student athletes continues.

The goal of community colleges and athletics programs should not be to maintain watered-down expectations to give the illusion that student athletes are truly being successful. Rather, the goal should be to set expectations that challenge and enable individuals to do their best at becoming the best student, athlete, and citizen they are capable of being. In order to properly assist student athletes to be the best they can be, institutions must find ways to transcend the negative perceptions and stereotypes their student athletes are confronted with on a daily basis.

Toward this end, the purpose of this chapter is to discuss the marginalization of student athletes and to (1) present data collected from case studies illustrating how institutions have been intentional in promoting student success and degree attainment for student athletes; and (2) highlight best practices used to empower, encourage, and support athletes. This chapter aims to provide institutions with pragmatic examples of programs and services that have been successful in creating institutional cultures that are dedicated to preparing student athletes to be competitive in the classroom and on the field of play. By highlighting these institutions, the author provides examples of ways institutions can work toward developing a culture that both challenges (i.e., maintain high expectations for student athletes' behavior) and supports (i.e., provide the necessary programs and services) student athletes to meet or surpass their own expectations, as well as the expectations of their respective institutions.

Student Athletes as Marginalized Students

In 2004, Berta Vigil Laden edited a volume of *New Directions for Community Colleges* in which several scholars and practitioners discussed how community colleges "recognize and respond to the academic, co-curricular, and cultural needs of their emerging majority student populations" (p. 1). The present chapter and NDCC volume builds on and advances Laden and colleagues' (2004) conversation. This is carried out through several focused discussions of student groups that have been historically marginalized within higher education, and more specifically at the community college. This chapter, in particular, focuses attention on student athletes as a marginalized group and the ways in which they are continually marginalized by institutions and members of the academic community.

Many may ask, what is a marginalized group, and how are student athletes marginalized? Previous scholarship has provided varying definitions of what a marginalized group is, as well as examples of ways in which this marginalization is manifested. These definitions and examples supply the rationale and justification for the inclusion of athletes within the conversation of marginalized groups. For instance, Kagan and colleagues (2004) suggest that marginalized people "have relatively little control over their lives and the resources available to them; they become stigmatized and are often at the receiving end of negative public attitudes" (p. 3). Sue (2010) defined marginalized groups and individuals as those that "are perceived negatively, given less status in society, and confined to existing on the margins of our social, cultural, political, and economic systems" (p. 5).

Furthermore, Kagan and colleagues (2004) discussed marginalization as a "shifting phenomenon linked to social status" (p. 2), in which certain individuals or groups enjoy at one point high social status, but when social change occurs, these same individuals may lose their status and become marginalized. As athletes, individuals are glamorized for their athletic performance in their given sport; but as students, they are vilified for their substandard academic abilities and their lack of focus and attention devoted to their academic studies (Simons et al., 2007). As such, student athletes are confronted with layered marginalization due to their status as a community college student, student athlete, and when applicable, as a member of an underrepresented ethnic, gender, or socioeconomic group.

This marginalization is carried out through microaggressions, which are "hidden demeaning messages that often lie outside of the level of conscious awareness of the perpetrators" (Sue, 2010, p. 4). For example, a coach might encourage an athlete to enroll in a course that is not listed on his degree program of study but will ensure an "A," rather than to enroll in a more rigorous course on the student's degree program plan of study that could impact his athletic eligibility if he does not successfully complete the course. The hidden message here is "I do not believe you are smart enough to successfully pass this course and your athletic eligibility is more important than your academic studies." Or a faculty member might say, "Don't worry about doing your homework for my class this semester because I know you have a busy athletic schedule." The hidden message: "No matter how hard you try, you will never pass my class so don't waste your time or mine. It is probably better to focus your time and attention on your athletic future."

These subtle and not-so-subtle messages reinforce the idea that student athletes are neither capable nor interested in their academic studies and further enforce negative stereotypes.

Methods: Case Selection and Sample

Data for this chapter were drawn from multiple sources to provide the richness and depth of each case description (Glesne, 1999). These methods included: (1) semistructured telephone interviews and (2) collection of Internet resources and primary documents from institutions regarding the goals and mission of their athletic program, student athletes' academic performance, and support services provided to student athletes. Data collection took place over an 11-month period, from November 2009 to October 2010. To identify case studies, Google alerts were created using the key words *community college* and *athletics* to capture local, regional, and national news articles pertaining to athletics at the community college level. Over the 11-month period, alerts were reviewed weekly, and a list was compiled of institutions that had been recognized for having high-performing student athletes. Independent Web searches were also conducted in addition to recommendations solicited from colleagues that work with or are familiar with exemplary-performing athletic programs.

From these initial steps, personnel at the selected institutions were contacted via e-mail and phone and invited to participate in a semistructured telephone interview. Five institutions were selected and agreed to participate. However, only one institution completed the study in its entirety.

Institutional Case Studies

Institutions were selected as case studies due to their record and focus on the academic success of student athletes at their respective institutions. For instance, during the 2009–2010 academic year, 24 student athletes from Owens College, located in Toledo, Ohio, received Academic All-Conference Honors by the Ohio Community College Athletic Conference ("News Releases," 2010). Likewise, over the past 12 years, Lake-Sumter Community College, in Leesburg, Florida, has had six athletes achieve NJCAA Distinguished Academic All-American Honors; 17 have been Academic All-Americans; and 115 former student athletes have made the FCCAA All-State Academic Team in their respective sports (Matulia, 2010). Between the fall 2006 and spring 2008 terms, 64 student athletes at Southwestern Illinois College (SWIC) earned an associate's degree (59) or certificate (5). During this same time period, student athletes at SWIC successfully earned 83 percent of the credit hours they attempted, and just over 34 percent of all athletes were selected for the academic honor roll.

Creating a Culture of Success: "Tradition Never Graduates". There are several essential aspects that must be present when developing an institutional culture that supports, encourages, and responds to the needs of student athletes. Part of building this culture is establishing a tradition of excellence. The development of a tradition of excellence is salient to the demarginalization of student athletes and altering the negative perceptions concerning their academic abilities and goals. During one of the interviews conducted for this study, an athletic director stated that at his institution "tradition never graduates." He further stated that "our tradition of academic integrity, our tradition of community and behavioral integrity, our athletic integrity . . . never graduates. . . . It [tradition] stays here and the next group has to live up to that same concept" (AD#1, 2010). The following section provides a discussion of some of the traditions that were identified at the examined case studies.

Integrity. Integrity should be at the center of any athletic program that strives to elevate the academic performance of its student athletes. A

NEW DIRECTIONS FOR COMMUNITY COLLEGES • DOI: 10.1002/cc

focus on integrity must encompass both academic and behavioral integrity. Programs with academic integrity place students' academic studies as paramount because they understand the benefit of students receiving a quality education and obtaining a degree or certificate. Such programs also take steps to ensure that students are advised properly and are taking courses that lead to a credential at the community college or to the ability to transfer to a four-year institution where they can complete a bachelor's degree. For these programs, meeting minimum requirements to maintain athletic eligibility is a product of the student's hard work in the classroom. Meeting these standards is not the ultimate goal, but surpassing them is. Such programs value athletic success, but not at the expense of the student's education.

Programs that have integrity recruit students of character and set high standards for student behavior both on and off the field. A coach at Lake-Sumter Community College noted, "We want student athletes with character and I believe that by stressing academics along with athletics, we can find those players" (Jolley, 2010, n.p.). Not only do programs with integrity set high standards for student conduct, but they hold students to these stated expectations. For instance, Southwestern Illinois College currently has a substance abuse policy in place that allows for the random drug testing of all student athletes. Though not common at most community colleges, this practice underscores this particular program's focus on protecting the integrity of the institution and athletic program and on the well-being of student athletes.

Teamwork.   It takes a community effort to build a tradition of excellence. First, coaches must be intent on recruiting quality students that are able to handle their academic and athletic responsibilities. The caliber of student athletes that are recruited by coaches demonstrates to the academic community the priorities of the athletic program. Second, athletic directors, coaches, administrators, and faculty must work together to develop program goals and academic support services for student athletes. Most often, it is the faculty that first notice potential academic problems with athletes. Maintaining an open line of communication with faculty will help with identifying students who are struggling academically or socially and can provide these students the assistance they need before the problem(s) become too severe.

Third, athletic programs should be open to involving parents and guardians in activities and conversations concerning their students' academic studies. Providing opportunities at the beginning of the academic year for parents, students, and athletic program staff to meet to discuss program goals and expectations can provide coaches additional support, as well as parents the opportunity to be involved in their students' success.

Commitment.   To truly develop a culture that supports and encourages student athletes' success takes a commitment on the part of the athletic program, institution, and student athlete. Athletic programs that are exemplary are committed to educating the whole student. They value the educational and athletic experience equally. Institutions that are committed to reversing negative perceptions of student athletes are committed to providing the best possible environment for learning to take place. This includes providing both human and financial support. And finally, students themselves must be committed to changing the negative stereotypes about student athletes by doing the right things in the classroom and in the community. If students are striving for excellence, the community will undoubtedly take notice.

Conclusion

A primary aim of this chapter was to discuss ways in which student athletes have been marginalized and provide recommendations for enhancing the experiences and academic outcomes of student athletes. The hope is that the presented information will inform practice, which will in turn help to decrease the marginalization of student athletes. When working with student athletes at the community college we would be wise to keep in mind the words of Johann W. Goethe. He suggested, "When we treat a man as he is, we make him worse than he is. When we treat him as if he already were what he potentially could be, we make him what he should be" (cited in Kerensky & Melby, 1975, p. 59).

References

Beilock, S. L., & McConnell, A. R. Stereotype threat and sport: Can athletic performance be threatened? *Journal of Sport & Exercise Psychology,* 2004, *26,* 597–609.

Glesne, C. Becoming qualitative researchers: An introduction (2nd ed.) New York: Longman, 1999.

Harrison, C. K. "Athleticated" versus educated: A qualitative investigation of campus perceptions, recruiting and African American male student-athletes. *Challenge Journal,* 2008, *14*(1), 39–60.

Jolley, F. True student-athletes. The Daily Commercial, 2010. Retrieved from www .dailycommercial.com/129LSCC.

Kagan, C., Burns, D., Burton, M., Crespo, I., Evans, R., et al. Working with people who are marginalized by the social system: Challenges for community psychological work, 2004. Retrieved from www.dehisi.org/upload/documentos/texts_equip/Kagan.pdf.

Kerensky, V. M., & Melby, E. O. Education II Revised: A social imperative. Midland, MI: Pendell, 1975.

Laden, B. V. (Ed.). Serving emerging majority students. *New Directions for Community Colleges, 127.* Hoboken, NJ: John Wiley & Sons, 2004.

Matulia, M. LSCC athletics. The Daily Commercial, 2010. Retrieved from www .dailycommercial.com/30college.

"News Releases." Owens express student-athletes named OCCAC 2009-10 academic all-conference, 2010. Retrieved from www.owens.edu/news_releases/?p=1619.

Purdy, D. A., Eitzen, S. D., & Hufnagel, R. Are athletes also students? The educational attainment of college athletes. *Social Problems,* 1982, *29*(4), 439–448.

Sailes, G. A. An investigation of campus stereotypes: The myth of the black athletic superiority and the dumb jock stereotype. *Sociology of Sport Journal,* 1993, *10,* 88–97.

Simons, H. D., Bosworth, C., Fujita, S., & Jensen, M. The athlete stigma in higher education. *College Student Journal,* 2007, *41*(2), 251–273.

Steele, C. M. A threat in the air: How stereotypes shape intellectual test performance of African Americans. *American Psychologist,* 1997, *52*(6), 613–629.

Sue, D. W. Microaggressions, marginality, and oppression: An introduction. In D. W. Sue (Ed.), *Microaggressions and marginality: Manifestation, dynamics, and impact.* Hoboken, NJ: John Wiley & Sons, 2010.

Watson, J. C. Overcoming the challenges of counseling college student athletes, 2003. Retrieved from ERIC (ED 475387).

DAVID HORTON, Jr., is an assistant professor in the Department of Counseling and Higher Education in the Patton College of Education and Human Services at Ohio University.

NEW DIRECTIONS FOR COMMUNITY COLLEGES • DOI: 10.1002/cc

4

Community colleges are among the most diverse institutions in the American higher education system. Students across lifestyles, creeds, racial/ethnic backgrounds, gender groups, ability levels, and socioeconomic status reflect the legacy of two-year institutions to provide educational opportunities for many on the margins of full participation. The preponderance of community college students seeks this tier of postsecondary education, as it promises to equalize educational access across divergent student populations. Nonetheless, the unique campus climates of community colleges have not halted marginalization that occurs for sexual minority students. In this chapter, the authors trace the dearth of available literature on LGBTQ students at community colleges, provide a commentary for future research, and offer action steps for practitioners in creating visibly inclusive LGBTQ campus environments.

A Primer on LGBTQ Students at Community Colleges: Considerations for Research and Practice

Eboni M. Zamani-Gallaher, Dibya Devika Choudhuri

For over a century, community colleges have provided pathways for postsecondary educational attainment for the masses, not just the elite members of the dominant culture. According to the American Association of Community Colleges (AACC), 43 percent of all undergraduate students enrolled in higher education attend a community college (AACC, 2009). With over 12 million students, community colleges are frequently the institutions of choice or the only postsecondary opportunity for students from underrepresented, marginalized groups. In fact, 45 percent of African American, 45 percent of Asian American, and over half of all Hispanic and Native American students in postsecondary education are at community colleges. Hence, two-year institutions have been commonly referred to as

NEW DIRECTIONS FOR COMMUNITY COLLEGES, no. 155, Fall 2011 © 2011 Wiley Periodicals, Inc.
Published online in Wiley Online Library (wileyonlinelibrary.com) • DOI: 10.1002/cc.456

the "people's college" and thought to represent "democracy's doors" allowing entry to participation in postsecondary education for those whose access has been limited (Cohen & Brawer, 2008).

The landscape of American college students is shifting, given changing demographics in society at large. Over two-fifths of first-generation college-going adults, 71 percent of students with disabilities, one-third of nontraditional age (i.e., 25+ years old), and roughly half of students age 50 years and older attend two-year institutions of higher learning (AACC, 2009; Barnett & Li, 1997). Community college students are more likely than their four-year counterparts to work full time, attend school part time, and have increased concerns regarding college costs (Zamani-Gallaher, Bazile, & Stevenson, in press).

Clearly, there is pluralism in the background characteristics of community college students. However, nearly 20 years have passed since Baker (1991) raised the first documented concern on the needs of homosexual students at two-year institutions. While the enrollment patterns for the aforementioned student populations have been well documented, what is known about LGBTQ students at community colleges is virtually nonexistent. Subsequently, this chapter endeavors to describe the limited literature on community college LGBTQ students.

LGBTQ Identity and Unlearning Falsehoods

Many myths surrounding homosexuality are often fueled by misinformation regarding sexual orientation in media portrayals (Besner & Spungin, 1995). Gay men are often portrayed as unable to commit, having difficulty with long-term relationships, shallow, obsessed with fashion, and always demonstrating effeminate characteristics. Lesbians are often rendered invisible or portrayed as witches, emasculating bullies, or tomboys with masculine characteristics (Barret & Logan, 2002). Bisexual and transgendered folk can be demonized or portrayed as freakish. The preceding stereotypes are pervasive and perpetuate homophobia in society and on college campuses.

For many marginalized groups, self-definition is important relative to establishing their collective identity on their own terms. In this chapter, we have intentionally opted to move beyond the conventional referencing to lesbian, gay, bisexual, and transgender as LGBT, to include the queer identifier. Work by Tierney (1997) and Rhoads (1994) contends that the identification of queer signals a "sense of pride and openness about one's same-sex desires as well as a degree of hostility toward heterosexism" (Rhoads, 1994, p. 3). Our conscious decision to utilize LGBTQ connotes our desire to release the muting of LGBTQ issues silenced within many two-year college environments. Additionally, given the multiplicity of identities and roles that community college students occupy (e.g., reentry single mother, displaced worker, senior citizen, traditional college-goers, etc.), we do not assume that there is a monolithic lived experience among LGBTQ folk. Nor do we assume that sexual identity is situated in a vacuum from the other microcultural group memberships to which students belong, construct meaning, or not occupy a segmented position in a different postsecondary educational context such as the community college (Zamani-Gallaher et al., in press). In sum, the term *queer* challenges heteronormativity and privileged positionality, providing a prism for examining student development across multiple identities (Abes & Kasch, 2007; Farell, Gupta, & Queen, 2005; Renn & Bilodeau, 2005). However, there is a wide variance in the literature in the use of terminology to reference these populations, and some shifts may occur as we report and review current literature.

Roughly five years ago, I (i.e., Zamani-Gallaher) found it particularly disconcerting to have one of my advisees employed at a community college as an academic advisor disclose her concerns over her colleagues' response to an openly gay student. This was the story she shared:

While sharing an office space with another advisor, she overheard the advisor's meeting with a student. The student shared that he had come out to his parents and had been kicked out of the house. He expressed his distress at being disowned by his parents and his inability to focus on studying for his final exams. Prior to this, he explained that he had maintained a solid B average throughout the semester. He wanted to know what his options were from the advisor. The advisor's response was, "Are you sure you are gay?" The student perplexedly replied that he had shared his coming out story only because he felt it was relevant background so she would not think he was just blowing off the final exam. The advisor then said, "I can assist you if you want out of this gayness. Otherwise, I can refer you to someone who can assist you, given that homosexuality contradicts my religious beliefs."

My student was not the only one disturbed by this exchange. It dawned on me to search for literature that pertained to LGBTQ students on two-year campuses after hearing about what I considered discriminatory. The literature search generated few writings related to LGBTQ students in community colleges. Ivory (2005) was among the couple of publications that could be located. In fact, Ivory stated, "fewer than six articles have been published regarding this population" (2005, p. 61). More distressing is that there have been no additional publications (i.e., empirical, theoretical, or applied) in the past five years since Ivory recommended that research is sorely absent to inform student affairs professionals on the need to further their understanding of sexual minorities at community colleges.

Negative LGBTQ Affect and Campus Climate Concerns

While a [nursing] student at a community college I was approached by my clinical instructor in my final semester and was asked: "Why are you a homosexual?" For several weeks after that encounter, it was like walking on eggshells. I received a copy of my mid-semester evaluation, it contained various references to my homosexuality and the potential problems associated with it, i.e., AIDS, STDs, potential attraction to patients of the same sex, and the potential for improper sexual conduct. (Renn, 2000, p. 131)

The preceding quote is one of the few negative exchanges documenting LGBTQ student in-class experiences at a community college. Institutional characteristics matter, and the need to know about the academic and social integration of LGBTQ students is critical to understanding their overall student satisfaction, psychosocial well-being, retention, and matriculation. For this reason, institutional type relative to the purposeful study of both two- and four-year campuses is a major oversight in the current literature. Community colleges and their students are often on the periphery of higher education (Townsend, Donaldson, & Wilson, 2005). However, two-year institutional contexts must be considered relevant in constructing knowledge about LGBTQ students and augmenting the extant literature. All told, the research examining institutional characteristics by institutional control (public or private), geographic variation, or special population colleges (i.e., historically Black colleges and universities; Hispanic-serving institutions of higher learning; tribal colleges; and single-sex institutions) is lacking.

In what can be considered the lone data-driven publication on LGBTQ and community colleges, 484 community college students were surveyed on homophobia (Franklin, 1998). While the unit of analysis still was not the LGBTQ student, cutting-edge research provided a glimpse into the hostile hallways that exist at two-year institutions. There are parallels that can be drawn between two- and four-year contexts as the challenges LGBTQ collegians face may not be mutually exclusive and bear some overlap.

The prevailing studies on campus climate for LGBTQ students is partial, as it narrowly addresses identity development, sexual harassment, violence, campus climate, and anti-affect toward LGBTQ with undergraduates at four-year colleges (Abes & Kasch, 2007; Evans, 2002; Rankin, 2003; Renn & Bilodeau, 2005; Rhoads, 1994; Sanlo, 2005; Wall & Evans, 1999; Wilkerson, Brooks, & Ross, 2010). Recently, at Houston Community College, a 29-year-old gay transgendered man, Lance Reyna. was believed to be the target of an armed robbery during Gay Pride week. He was approached in the restroom by the assailant and told, "Hey queer, I need you to be quiet, cooperate, and give me all your valuables." Reyna fought back and was beaten, suffering a concussion (Cerota, 2010).

In April 2009, student leaders at American River College in Sacramento, California, passed a resolution opposing a nationally organized day of silent demonstration in support of gay rights. The resolution states that the demonstration was an attempt to intimidate and harass religious students from expressing their views on homosexuality. Following the passage, students galvanized in response to the antigay religious coalition, subsequently voting the right-wing religious conservative students at the community college out of office.

The inadequate coverage of open hostility against LGBTQ students at community colleges engenders a lack of awareness about the campuses with hostile hallways and the campus climates that are laudable in their efforts to have inclusive climates. The 2010 Campus Pride LGBT-Friendly Campus Climate Index Report of Colleges is a national assessment tool comprised of over 50 self-assessment questions for institutions interested in promoting a welcoming environment for LGBTQ students (this report uses *LGBT* as the term of choice and in the interests of accuracy, we conform to this terminology in reviewing the report). The assessment aligns with eight different LGBT-friendly factors (i.e., LGBT policy inclusion, LGBT support and institutional commitment, LGBT student life, LGBT academic life, LGBT housing, LBGT campus safety, LGBT counseling and health, and LGBT recruitment and retention) (Campus Pride, 2010). Each of the 237 institutions profiled are rated using a five-star scoring system, with a five-star rating reflective of progressive campuses with inclusive policies, programs, and practices for LGBT students. Only 12 of the 237 institutions cataloged are community colleges. Averaging a mean rating of two out of five stars, six of the 12 community colleges are located in small cities in five different states with 5,000 to 6,000 students. Two of the community colleges are in large urban areas—one with 3,000 students, ranking two out of five stars on the East Coast, and the other on the West Coast with 18,000 students coming in at four out of five stars. The remaining four featured in the LGBT Campus Climate Index are situated in medium-sized cities, with three institutions in the Midwest averaging two out of five stars, while the only medium-sized community college rating four out of five stars was on the West Coast.

Also of note, Campus Pride conducted the first national study of LGBT students slated for release in fall 2010. Item 33 of the questionnaire asks whether students attend a two- or four-year college. Two-hundred fifty-three collegians indicated attending a two-year institution, representing 4.9 percent of those responding (S. Rankin, personal communication, August 13, 2010). However, it is not discernable whether student respondents were concurrently enrolled at both two- and four-year colleges or if there had been vertical or reverse transfer among respondents that may shape their perceptions of campus climate for LGBT students (S. Rankin, personal communication, September 6, 2010). It is questionable whether community college leaders desire to advance caring-inclusive, LGBTQ climates at their respective campuses. There are more than 100 LGBT resource centers staffed at four-year colleges in Canada and the United States. In contrast, a single, formally staffed LGBT resource center exists at a community college (National Consortium of Directors of LGBT Resources in Higher Education, 2005 as cited by Villareal, 2009). Not surprisingly, it is dubious whether there are safe spaces on two-year campuses.

Only 7 of 219 colleges that offer a safe zone or allies program are community colleges (Tubbs, 2005). In a recent review of the AACC web site, using the search term *LGBTQ*, merely seven results were generated, three of which correspond with the forthcoming Welcoming Community Colleges Initiatives sponsored by the Academy for Educational Development, the Human Rights Campaign, and the National Council on Student Development. The collaborative is four-pronged, seeking to:

1. Increase awareness and build a baseline of knowledge of institutional policies, practices, and partnerships that promote or detract from LGBT students' educational success.
2. Identify and address barriers for strengthening postsecondary outcomes for LGBT community college students.
3. Develop technical assistance tools and guidance that will help to promote and sustain institutional change.
4. Implement and evaluate a model of policies, practices, and partnerships that create a Welcoming Community College (Welcoming Community Colleges Initiative, 2008, p. 2).

From Theory to Practice: Sexual Identity Development and Student Support Services

One of the important aspects of having a theoretical underpinning for services offered to any category of student is that it can inform us about our underlying assumptions that in turn infuse the services we offer. Most student services offered to sexual minority students have been framed in sexual identity formation theory, but focusing on the coming-out process as proposed by Cass (Reynolds & Hanjorgiris, 2000). In the best known of these models, Cass (1979) identified six stages of a common gay and lesbian identity formation that moved from a pregay to a gay identity through the stages of confusion, comparison, tolerance, acceptance, pride, and synthesis. This model was derived from clinical and empirical data and grounded in interpersonal congruency theory, assuming that identity was acquired through a developmental process, and that the locus lay in the interaction process between persons and their environment. However, a critique of models such as this was for subsuming lesbian identity development under the rubric of gay identity and being based primarily on data from White, middle-aged males (Barret & Logan, 2002). Weinberg, Williams, and Pryor (1994) proposed a model of bisexual identity development based on three stages. Yet no empirically derived model has been proposed to account for the complicated process of moving through transgender identity development.

As mentioned by Ivory (2005), the coming-out process has been seen as crucial for LGBTQ students. However, this assumption is based on a developmental model of a traditional-aged student, leaving home for the first time, in the stages of moving through late adolescence into provisional early adulthood. Developmental tasks of differentiation and the Eriksonian task of identity assumption versus identity confusion are associated with college students.

A significant portion of the community college population consists of students in a position such as the aforementioned. However, there are also important populations of students who are in very different life stages than traditional-age collegians (i.e., 18–24 years of age). For example, there are students firmly in adulthood who are juggling full-time work, parenthood, and academics, as well as students in middle adulthood who are returning for retraining and new skill attainment after being out of the workforce. Thus, the spaces they occupy in the sexual identity development continuum will be very different, with a need for different kinds of services. It seems necessary to account for the complexity and diversity of needs with a theoretical framework that is as complex.

A multidimensional model of sexual identity development developed by Worthington, Savoy, Dillon, and Vernaglia (2002) demonstrates the complexity of these processes for all persons even though the model focuses on heterosexual identity development. The model incorporates six biopsychosocial influences and six dimensions of individual identity, which interact with aspects of group membership identity and attitudes toward sexual minorities. In this model, Worthington et al. (2002) distinguish between sexual identity as a comprehensive process regarding one's identity as a sexual being versus sexual orientation identity regarding acceptance and recognition of one's sexual orientation. The biopsychosocial dimensions include biological factors, the microsocial context, gender norms and socialization, culture, and religious orientation, as well as the systemic homonegativity and sexual prejudice toward LGBTQ populations.

More pertinently to the community college student population, the model also describes an interactive developmental process that can occur both consciously and unconsciously at all stages in the model, and is not linear in progression through stages or tied to any specific age: (1) *unexplored commitment,* describing acceptance of microsocial and societal mandates for prescribed gender and sexual behavior roles and avoidance of sexual self-exploration; (2) *active exploration,* where there is purposeful exploration, evaluation, or experimentation (cognitive, affective, or behavioral) of sexual needs, values, orientation, or preferences for activities, characteristics in partners, or sexual expression; (3) *diffusion,* which may resemble the active exploration but lacks goal-directed intentionality, and is more likely to be chaotic or reactive and often arises from crisis; moving to (4) *deepening and commitment* as needs, values, modes, and expressions of sexual preferences and characteristics are identified; and (5) *synthesis,* characterized by congruence and consistency between both individual identity and development. Using the Worthington et al. (2002) Sexual Identity Model, we contend that educators and counselors can take action

Table 4.1.   Choudhuri & Zamani-Gallaher Modification of Sexual
Identity Development: Considerations for College Student Personnel

Developmental Stage	Student Needs/Challenges	Student Personnel Actions/Services
Unexplored commitment	Social image and roles	Information, welcoming environment Invitations for exploration and learning
Active exploration	Social networking and connections; silence, invisibility, obstacles, and secrets	Socialization opportunities Support groups Clubs and social organizations Faculty and staff models, mentors, and allies
Diffusion	Discrimination; broken relationships	Hate crimes protocols and policies Supportive services Counseling services
Deepening and commitment	Leadership opportunities and advocacy	Student leadership training Social organizations Connecting academic and personal passion
Synthesis	Disconnect with self and learning	Academic projects that utilize personal learning Opportunities to teach and lead

and provide targeted services that align with the needs and challenges facing LGBTQ students at community college campuses. Table 4.1 presents preliminary actions and services that can integrate with the various stages of the sexual identity development process. Please note that a more exhaustive list of action steps are offered later in this chapter.

Petitioning Future Research

There is a clear need for increased research on LGBTQ students. To understand the educational and supportive needs of LGBTQ students, it is essential to have empirical data that is demographic, historical, and longitudinal. Many LGBTQ students choose not to identify themselves as such in student surveys and on campus forms. As more surveys and forms commonly include questions on sexual orientation and gender identity, and campuses protect students' privacy, LGBTQ students may be more responsive and identify themselves more readily.

Renn (2010) argues that the available literature on LGBTQ in higher education is short on theoretical and methodological muster in addition to failing to apply queer theory as a useful lens to understand the realities of LGBTQ students. However, although Renn felt that the bulk of studies were

NEW DIRECTIONS FOR COMMUNITY COLLEGES • DOI: 10.1002/cc

campus climate related, she contends climate studies are still necessary. This is especially true of climate studies that look across multiple identities, infuse globalization, and employ large-scale survey research methods. Nonetheless, the research on LGBTQ folk, their challenges, and concerns is so scant that, arguably, more research, whether quantitative or qualitative on campus climate, on identity, or attitudinal related, should be welcomed.

Choudhuri (2003) suggests, "Social identities are complex and multiple, intersecting with each other as with the context and the shifting meanings ascribed to them by both the perceiver and the perceived" (p. 270). Given the relative absence or superficial treatment of bisexual and transgender students in general, this suggests a strong case for qualitative research in particular to ascertain their experiences. Moreover, given the diverse students at community colleges, it is open to question if LGBTQ student development can be understood divorced from other aspects of identity such as age, class, disability, ethnicity, gender, nationality, race, and religion (Berila & Choudhuri, 2005).

Professionals serious about constructing a climate of care for sexual minority students can take a crack at securing external funding for LGBTQ programming on their campus. By undertaking grant writing opportunities, there can be initial funding for sponsoring professional development initiatives, action research, and to establish improved support services at two-year institutions. This could initiate a paradigm shift from silence and invisibility to campuses that echo ethos of care for sexual minorities. One such source is the LGBTQ Funders organization that provides a searchable database and online directory of funding agents supporting work on LGBTQ issues. Additionally, through securing outside funding, administrators, faculty, and staff committed to creating climates of inclusion for LGBTQ students could also embark on practitioner scholarship by engaging in action research that would generate best practices in student services for LGBTQ collegians to be shared with other two-year college educators.

Stepping Up Student Support Services for LGBTQ Collegians

In community colleges, the response to sexual minority student needs has often been a resounding silence. Even though there may be a student organization on campus or an office that addresses those needs, LGBTQ student services mostly tend to be absent rather than present in two-year colleges (Ivory, 2005). Student support services at community colleges must move beyond striving to duplicate and offer services akin to those at traditional four-year institutions in several ways. As pointed out previously, the composition of students at two-year institutions is different, bringing unique needs and requiring a more multifaceted, complex set of responses. In most cases, many of these responses are already present, though applied differently than to LGBTQ students.

A case in point is that many community colleges actively respond to the needs of commuter students who interact on campus for short periods rather than having a residential tenure. Technological advances have allowed some community college students to engage actively online as institutions have created an online presence (e.g., via advertising, registration, orientation, and online course offerings). As a result, students can join in the campus community remotely from wherever they are rather than only engaging in person or extracting a sense of community that requires being on campus. For LGBTQ students, this can be a fortunate thing. If the college web site addresses LGBTQ issues openly and accessibly, there is a sense of welcome. Both heterosexual and LGBTQ students will get the message about the stance of the institution that in turn leads to greater openness and safety in the overall environment.

One advantage of the benefits of technology is that students who are in the early stages of coming out or who are heterosexual but have LGBTQ friends can access information that will be helpful in their identity formation without in any way judging or steering their development. Similar to fact sheets and FAQs developed on other topics, the web site can offer dedicated links to the coming-out process, socialization experiences, available supportive services, services for allies, and so on. Additionally, while face-to-face socializing opportunities are necessary, online interaction offers anonymity and safety. If there is space available for listservs or dedicated blogs, students may participate in much higher numbers than if they have to publicly congregate in an observable location. Given the composite and age-varied nature of students attending two-year institutions, socialization opportunities need to be varied. Evening events may not work for those with family responsibilities, while those who commute long distances may prefer events that can be scheduled around their class times.

One way to break the silence on sexual orientation and its accompanying social messages, confusions, and reactivity is to frame an institutional statement of inclusion and acceptance. This should be accompanied with a well-understood protocol for dealing with incidents of discrimination and hatred. Before incidents happen, student affairs administrators should be confident in their approach and the policies. It is important that such policies should not be solely judicial in their scope and approach, but involve means of communicating to the institutional community, spreading messages of acceptance that contradict any discriminatory reactions, as well as respond affirmatively to programs and educational initiatives. This is of great benefit not just to LGBTQ students who may be impacted, but also to students of diverse identities who may have been impacted by oppression and read the messages sent by the institution as broadly affirming.

Students who have come to an understanding of their identity and comfort are often passionate advocates and strong leaders if given the opportunity to become involved. Training for student leaders that addresses diversity leadership and welcoming their involvement while supporting

Table 4.2. Action Steps for Supporting LGBTQ at Community Colleges

Institutional Commitment	Faculty/Staff/Community Involvement	Student Success
Develop institutional nondiscrimination statements and implement anti-harassment policies if absent. Draft a diversity goal statement that addresses sexual orientation and identity. Create an ad-hoc committee to assess the campus culture; conduct regular environmental scans; develop a visible mission statement that illustrates the institutional commitment to diversity along the spectrum of difference, acknowledging the multiplicity of collegiate identities intersecting with queer identity.	Advocate for academic and social student engagement that improve the quality of life for LGBTQ persons on campus. Acknowledge heteronormative assumptions and challenge heterosexist structural inequities at your campus. Encourage faculty to teach content that embeds the contributions of the LGBTQ community. Sponsor professional development in-services and/or conferences for community college faculty and staff that raise awareness, increase allies, and dismantle chilly campus climates for LGBTQ students. Establish learning opportunities that call for increased cultural competencies among community college educators.	Recognize and address LGBTQ students from first entry, in developing recruitment, admission, and orientation materials in print, publicity, and Web-based services. Provide support for LGBTQ student leadership beyond the borders of campus. Originate leadership development opportunities for LGBTQ students, and/or sponsor student participation at state/national student leadership summits.

New Directions for Community Colleges • DOI: 10.1002/cc

Table 4.2. (Continued)

Institutional Commitment	Faculty/Staff/Community Involvement	Student Success
Develop and articulate strategic planning initiatives being purposeful in establishing a commitment to student development inclusive of LGBTQ issues together with promoting the holistic development of other diverse student groups.	Among available openly gay faculty and staff, establish an LGBTQ mentoring program to give LGBTQ community college students accessible role models on campus to provide emotional support alongside educational and career guidance for successfully navigating higher education as an LGBTQ collegian.	Incorporate diverse programming inclusive of sexual minorities by setting up an LGBTQ speakers bureau. Focus on programs, events, and activities that remove the veil of invisibility and silence.
Dedicate human and fiscal resources in the form of a stand-alone LGBTQ Resource Center or Office for LGBTQ Affairs.	Integrate LGBTQ issues into the general education curriculum and special topic queer studies courses; offer programs such as webinars and noncredit courses through continuing education as fitting.	Encourage a visible presence and acknowledgment of LGBTQ individuals on community college campuses (e.g., through bulletin board displays, fact sheets, historical timeline of gay rights, passing out gay-straight/ally pins, rainbow stickers during student activities events, etc.).
Advocate and champion for inclusion of LGBTQ matters among educational policy makers (e.g., state boards of trustees, AACC board of directors, Department of Education—Adult, etc.) in breaking the veneer of invisibility pertaining to issues of access, equity, and social justice for LGBTQ individuals in the two-year college context.	Start an institutional listserv to distribute relevant information from the research, practitioner, and policy communities that serve to promote full inclusion. This site can serve as the hub for useful links, white papers, policy briefs, best practices, working support groups, local social services, and a bibliography of readings on LGBTQ concerns, among other sources of information.	Encourage social networking, listservs, and/or blogs for LGBTQ individuals and their supporters to connect regarding campus life, workplace issues, college climate concerns, and collaboration on raising awareness.

their efforts is a critical piece in fostering lifelong leaders. The student leader, the student population, the institution, and the community will benefit from efforts in this area.

Some returning adult students may be perfectly content to have socialization opportunities in their home communities, while seeing the college solely as a site for learning. Here is where having faculty and staff allies who can assist with projects, as well as mentor and advise students on ways to combine their personal lives with their new learning, can be extremely beneficial. They serve as role models and can be extremely influential in the life of a student, sometimes making a significant impact on the retention and success of a student. Mature students' life experiences, when respected and incorporated into their new learning, can make significant differences in their ability to be confident and competent, as well as make them feel that they are connecting the various pieces of their life toward integration rather than diffusion.

Under every circumstance, leadership ought to be in front, taking on an activist stance to respond to need (Zamani-Gallaher, Green, Brown, & Stovall, 2009). Hence, college student personnel need to think "OUTside" of the box in meeting the needs of LGBTQ students that have gone unnoticed in the literature and in many community college environments. We have outlined action steps in Table 4.2 illustrating the necessity for institutional, faculty, staff, and administrative commitments to foster inclusive campus climates.

Conclusion

The existing literature on LGBTQ students largely documents sexual identity development of students on four-year campuses. To date, there are no published studies that squarely focus on LGBTQ students who attend community colleges. More specifically, literature that explores the viewpoints, reflections, coping strategies, and the impact that community colleges have in shaping the experiences of LGBTQ students on two-year campuses is nonexistent.

Community college personnel should call to question how they could be increasingly responsive, reflective practitioners in meeting the needs of marginalized student populations at two-year institutions. Considerations for increasing individual and institutional levels of support for LGBTQ matters on campus can be actualized through the creation of an action plan that instills personal and college accountability for improving the climate and sense of community afforded to LGBTQ students.

References

Abes, E. S., & Kasch, D. Using queer theory to explore lesbian college students' multiple dimensions of identity. *Journal of College Student Development*, 2007, 48(6), 619–636.

American Association of Community Colleges. *Factsheet*. Washington, DC: American Association of Community Colleges, 2009.

Baker, J. A. Gay nineties: Addressing the needs of the homosexual community and junior college students and faculty. *Community/Junior College*, 1991, *15*(1), 25–32.

Barnett, L., & Li, Y. *Disability support services in community colleges: Research brief* (ACC-RB-97-I). Washington, DC: American Association of Community Colleges, 1997.

Barret, B., & Logan, C. *Counseling gay men and lesbians: A practice primer.* Pacific Grove, CA: Brooks/Cole, 2002.

Berila, B., & Choudhuri, D. D. Metrosexuality the middle class way: Exploring race, class and gender in "Queer Eye for the Straight Guy." *Genders Online Journal*, 2005, 42.

Besner, H. F., & Spungin, C. I. *Gay and lesbian students: Understanding their needs.* Washington, DC: Taylor Francis, 1995.

Campus Pride LGBT-friendly campus climate index: National assessment tool. Charlotte, NC: Campus Pride, 2010.

Cass, V. C. Homosexual identity formation: A theoretical model. *Journal of Homosexuality*, 1979, *4*(30), 219–235.

Cerota, A. Gay student who was beaten speaks out. Houston, TX: KTRK TV/DT. Retrieved on July 9, 2010, from abclocal.go.com/ktrk/story?section=news/local&id=7523020&pt=print"pt=print, 2010, June 26.

Choudhuri, D. D. Qualitative research and multicultural counseling competency: An argument for inclusion. In D. B. Pope-Davis (Ed.), *Handbook of multicultural competencies in counseling and psychology* (pp. 267–282). Thousand Oaks, CA: Sage, 2003.

Cohen, A. M., & Brawer, F. B. *The American community college* (5th ed.). San Francisco, CA: Jossey-Bass, 2008.

Evans, N. J. The impact of an LGBT safe zone project on campus climate. *Journal of College Student Development*, 2002, *43*, 522–539.

Farell, K., Gupta, N., & Queen, M. (Eds.). Interrupting heteronormativity: Lesbian, gay, bisexual, and transgender pedagogy and responsible teaching at Syracuse University. Syracuse, NY: Syracuse University, 2005.

Franklin, K. *Psychological motivations of hate crimes perpetrators: Implications for educational intervention.* Paper presented at the 106th Annual Convention of the American Psychological Association, San Francisco, California (ED 423 939), 1998.

Ivory, B. T. LGBT students in community college: Characteristics, challenges, and recommendations. *New Direction for Student Services*, 2005, *11*, 62–69.

Rankin, S. *Campus climate for gay, lesbian, bisexual and transgender people: A national perspective*. Cambridge, MA: National Gay and Lesbian Task Force Policy Institute, 2003.

Renn, K. A. Including all voices in the classroom: Teaching lesbian, gay, and bisexual students. *College Teaching*, 2000, *48*(4), 129–135.

Renn, K. A. LGBT and queer research in higher education: The state and status of the field. *Educational Researcher*, 2010, *39*(2), 132–141.

Renn, K. A., & Bilodeau, B. Queer student leaders: An exploratory case study of identity development and LGBT student involvement at a Midwestern research university. *Journal of Gay & Lesbian Issues in Education*, 2005, *2*(4), 49–71.

Reynolds, A. L., & Hanjorgiris, W. F. Coming out: Lesbian, gay, and bisexual identity development. In R. M. Perez, K. A. DeBord, & K. J. Bieschke (Eds.), *Handbook of counseling and psychotherapy with lesbian, gay, and bisexual clients* (pp. 35–55). Washington, DC: American Psychological Association, 2000.

Rhoads, R. A. Coming out in college: The struggle for a queer identity. Westport, CT: Bergin & Garvey, 1994.

Sanlo, R. L. Lesbian, gay, and bisexual college students: Risk, resiliency, and retention. *Journal of College Student Retention*, 2005, *6*(1), 97–110.

Tierney, W. G. Academic outlaws: Queer theory and cultural studies in the academy. Thousand Oaks, CA: Sage Publications, 1997.

Townsend, B. K., Donaldson, J., & Wilson, T. Marginal or monumental? Visibility of community colleges in selected higher-education journals. *Community College Journal of Research and Practice*, 2005, 29(2), 123–135.

Tubbs, N. J. *Safe zone/allies programs: Campuses which offer a safe zone or allies program.* Retrieved on July 31, 2010, from www.lgbtcampus.org/old_faq/safe_zone _roster.html, 2005.

Villareal, H. B. (2009, February). Welcoming community colleges initiative: Supporting educational and labor market success for lesbian, gay, bisexual, and transgendered students. National Council on Student Development Newsletter. Retrieved from http://www.ncsdonline.org/pdf/2009winter.pdf.

Wall, V. A., & Evans, N. J. (Eds.). *Toward acceptance: Sexual orientation issues on campus.* Lanham, MD: University Press of America, 1999.

Weinberg, M. S., Williams, C. J., & Pryor, D. W. *Dual attractions: Understanding bisexuality.* New York, NY: Oxford University Press, 1994.

Welcoming Community Colleges Initiative. *Supporting educational and labor market success for lesbian, gay, bisexual, and transgender students: A concept paper.* Retrieved on August 1, 2010 from www.aacc.nche.edu/Resources/aaccprograms/accessinclusion /Documents/welcomingccs_112008.pdf.

Wilkerson, J. M., Brooks, A. K., & Ross, M. W. Sociosexual identity development and sexual risk taking of acculturating collegiate gay and bisexual men. *Journal of College Student Development*, 2010, 51(3), 279–296.

Worthington, R. L., Savoy, H. B., Dillon, F. R., & Vernaglia, E. R. Heterosexual identity development: A multidimensional model of individual and social identity. *The Counseling Psychologist*, 2002, 30, 496–531.

Zamani-Gallaher, E. M., Bazile, S., & Stevenson, T. N. Segmentation, capital, and community college transfer students: Exploring community colleges as agents of currency. In R. D. Bartee (Ed.), *Contemporary perspectives on capital in educational contexts.* Charlotte, NC: Information Age, in press.

Zamani-Gallaher, E. M., Green, D. O., Brown, M. C., & Stovall, D. O. *The case for affirmative action on campus: Concepts of equity, considerations for practice.* Sterling, VA: Stylus Publishing, 2009.

EBONI M. ZAMANI-GALLAHER is a professor of educational leadership and coordinator of the Community College Leadership Program in the Department of Leadership and Counseling at Eastern Michigan University.

DIBYA DEVIKA CHOUDHURI is an associate professor in the Department of Leadership and Counseling at Eastern Michigan University.

5

This chapter will identify ways in which community colleges are well positioned to support student veterans, discuss the need for heightened awareness concerning student veterans' experiences, and make recommendations to assist staff, faculty, and administrators to better serve student veterans at their institutions.

Student Veterans and Community Colleges

Corey Rumann, Marisa Rivera, Ignacio Hernandez

Higher Education and the Military

Higher education and the military have been linked throughout U.S. history. This relationship began with the Morrill Act of 1862, which mandated military training as part of the curriculum at land grant institutions (Abrams, 1989; Neiberg, 2000). Veterans have also impacted higher education by enrolling in college following military service. Their influence was especially relevant with the introduction of the Servicemen's Readjustment Act of 1944—popularly known as the GI Bill—when many veterans of World War II took advantage of the financial incentives provided by the GI Bill and entered or returned to college (Olson, 1973, 1974). At that time, the number of veterans returning or entering college was unprecedented and nearly overwhelmed colleges and universities.

The Post 9/11 GI Bill.   The latest version of the GI Bill—the Post 9/11 GI Bill—was enacted on August 1, 2009. This iteration of the GI Bill offers more generous and expanded benefits for qualifying veterans to attend college (Cook & Kim, 2009; U.S. Department of Veterans Affairs, 2009a). Indeed, student veterans are expected to enroll in college in numbers unprecedented since the aftermath of World War II (Cook & Kim, 2009; Moltz, 2009; Radford, 2009). These benefits more adequately cover the full costs of a college education, including higher stipends for books and expenses in addition to tuition for some student veterans depending on their particular situations and circumstances (U.S. Department of Veterans Affairs, 2009b). For example, the Post 9/11 GI Bill will cover the costs of tuition up to the highest tuition charged at the state's public institutions

New Directions for Community Colleges, no. 155, Fall 2011 © 2011 Wiley Periodicals, Inc.
Published online in Wiley Online Library (wileyonlinelibrary.com) • DOI: 10.1002/cc.457

(U.S. Department of Veterans Affairs, 2009b). In addition, programs such as the Yellow Ribbon Program offer veterans more flexibility in where they choose to attend college (Eckstein, 2009; Redden, 2009). Through the Yellow Ribbon program the federal government will match dollar for dollar whatever institutions are willing to contribute toward tuition costs that are not covered by GI Bill funding (U.S. Department of Veterans Affairs, 2009b). While it was thought that the increased flexibility might lead to more student veterans enrolling at four-year public and private institutions, that may not be the case (Sewall, 2010). Additionally, private, for-profit institutions tend to enroll higher numbers of student veterans than all other types of institutions (Sewall, 2010).

Student Veterans and Community Colleges

Following World War II, the President's Commission on Higher Education released *Higher Education for American Democracy*, popularly known as the Truman Commission Report of 1946. It called for, among other things, the establishment of a network of public community colleges that would charge little or no tuition, serve as cultural centers, be comprehensive in their program offerings with emphasis on civic responsibilities, and serve the area in which they were located. The community college played an integral role, perhaps larger than any other segment of higher education, in the postwar demographic expansion of American institutions of higher education (Brint & Karabel, 1989). The year 1944 is a landmark in the history of the relationship of community colleges and the military. The GI Bill helped shape a middle class in the United States, by furthering social mobility through access to higher education. It must not be ignored, however, that the bill was written "almost exclusively for Whites" (Katznelson, 2005, p. 114). The GI Bill was written and sponsored by southern congressmen and intentionally designed to support separate-but-equal Jim Crow laws (Katznelson, 2005).

The ability of community colleges to respond to constituent needs makes them ideal spaces to enroll student veterans. An array of baccalaureate, prebaccalaureate, and vocational course options are available at almost all community colleges. Technological advances in course delivery methods may also be an ideal choice for student veterans with commitments on military installations or bases. Distance learning technologies may increase community colleges' capacity as well as help to accommodate student veteran enrollment growth.

Addressing the Needs of Student Veterans at Community Colleges. The growth in the number of veterans entering higher education as well as the expanded Post 9/11 GI Bill has brought about competition among colleges and universities redund for student veterans. In addition to the Post 9/11 GI Bill, many colleges and universities are also creating programs that offer veterans additional financial aid to attend their institution. For example, "The Ohio GI Promise" program ensures that veterans will receive the in-state tuition rate regardless of their official residence. This translates into a cost savings of $13,000 a year for a student veteran, which the state of Ohio hopes will encourage veterans to consider relocating to attend school and use their Post 9/11 GI Bill benefits (University System of Ohio, n.d.). New York State also announced a Veterans Tuition Award (VTA) (New York State Division of Veterans Affairs, 2010). This program is for eligible veterans pursuing a degree in New York State. The VTA can potentially reduce tuition by 98 percent (New York State Division of Veterans Affairs, 2010). While these programs may cater to four-year institutions and/or vocational schools, it is important to note that many of these schools have entered into articulation agreements that facilitate transferring from a community college into a college or university.

Several community colleges across the country have implemented programs focused specifically on student veterans. Citrus College (California) opened a veterans' center in 2009 that offers student veterans a space where they can come together and relax as well as find out about resources, make copies, use computers, attend workshops, and buy snacks (Chappell, 2010). Additionally, Citrus College offers a course that assists student veterans in the transition from military to civilian life or from deployment to postdeployment life (Chappell, 2010; Quillen-Armstrong, 2007). The course—Boots to Books—teaches student veterans interpersonal skills and helps them manage the stressors they may encounter during their transition from military to civilian life (Quillen-Armstrong, 2007). Community colleges are also offering orientation programs designed specifically for student veterans. Danville Area Community College (Illinois) hosted a Veteran's Community Resource Orientation that offered returning military veterans information regarding employment, education, health, and support services (Chappell, 2010).

A trend among colleges and universities is the creation of Student Veterans of America (SVA) organizations on their campuses. This national organization was founded in 2008 with the primary purpose of providing peer-to-peer networks, connecting student veterans to resources, and advocating on their behalf (Student Veterans of America, 2008). The SVA not only coordinates campus activities for the student veterans but also provide preprofessional networking and a familiar point of contact at each student veteran's specific institution. The SVA plays an important role in the success of student veterans in higher education. Interestingly, the number of community colleges with an official SVA is outnumbered by four-year institutions with an SVA organization nearly 4 to 1 (J. Glastetter, personal communication, June 6, 2010).

In 1972 the Servicemembers Opportunity Colleges (SOC) was established with the purpose of creating and coordinating programs for service members and their families (Ford, Northrup, & Wiley, 2009). The SOC collaborates with national organizations to improve educational support for student veterans. Schools partnering with SOC accept transfer credit from other SOC member institutions that allows the students being deployed or relocated to maximize his or her access to higher education. Presently, the SOC has approximately 1,900 institutional members, many of which are community colleges (Servicemembers Opportunity Colleges, 2010).

A recently released report provides important information concerning services and programs provided by institutions of higher education, including community colleges (Cook & Kim, 2009). Data was collected from 723 institutions of higher education and indicated that 57 percent of those responding provided some sort of programs and services to student veterans. The report also highlights, however, that the services are not always all inclusive or provided by a designated office. Often, the services are offered by offices that also serve the typical student. This is especially true at community colleges. Overall, the report states that since September 11, 2001, 65 percent of community colleges have renewed their focus on ensuring that the needs of student veterans are met.

Student affairs practitioners at community colleges should recognize the value in addressing the physical, psychological, social, and academic needs of student veterans. Entering, or reentering, a postsecondary program of study is a daunting task for anyone, no less for veterans returning from war zones. Many community colleges are addressing the needs of student veterans through policies and programs; however, more needs to be done to help support this unique student population. One of the challenges is the lack of information currently available regarding the student veteran experience at community colleges and assessments of services offered that focus on the needs of student veterans. The next section of this chapter will discuss what we currently know about student veterans' experiences.

The Student Veteran Experience.   Increasingly more and more studies are investigating the experiences of contemporary student veterans in U.S. higher education (Bauman, 2009; DiRamio, Ackerman, & Mitchell, 2008; Persky & Oliver, 2010; Rumann, 2010; Rumann & Hamrick, 2010; Sargent, 2009); however, only two have focused on community college students (Persky & Oliver, 2010; Rumann, 2010). This research begins to help student affairs professionals and administrators understand student veteran experiences on college and university campuses and the types of programs, services, and strategies that might help ease their transitions. Still, more research needs to be done to gain a clearer understanding of this unique student population.

Student veterans likely experience a sudden change in environments when enrolling in college following active-duty military service (Rumann & Hamrick, 2010). Adjusting to the less structured nature of the college environment can be challenging—especially initially—for some student veterans who have grown accustomed to the structured daily routine in the military. In addition, for some student veterans, concerns about how they might be perceived by others can complicate the transition process and compel them to conceal their veteran identity in some situations, including on campus (DiRamio et al., 2008). Student veterans' voices may not be heard as they negotiate the difficult transition process of going to college, and their adjustment—both academically and socially—can be affected.

Student veterans have also disclosed feeling disconnected from their nonmilitary college student peers who do not seem to have a realistic sense of the military operations in Iraq and Afghanistan. This disconnect is further influenced by the civilian population's inability to relate to the military experiences of veterans. Consequently, veterans may be asked questions such as "So, did you kill anyone over there?" Nonmilitary students (and others) may seek to understand those experiences in insensitive ways, which—while unintentional—has a potentially negative effect on student veterans and their transitions (Bauman, 2009; DiRamio et al., 2008; Rumann & Hamrick, 2010; Rumann, 2010). This disconnect, along with perceived immaturity on the part of some students (Persky & Oliver, 2010), may make it difficult for student veterans to find sources of support in the community college environment, further complicating their social and academic adjustment. Consequently, student veterans tend to seek out other veterans to help ease their transitions because other veterans are able to relate to their experiences (Rumann, 2010; Rumann & Hamrick, 2010). Indeed, student veterans appreciate opportunities to meet and interact with other veterans on campus that can help make the college environment feel less isolating and help ease their adjustment.

Faculty members also play a key role in how student veterans perceive the campus environment. Student veterans in one study reported that faculty members were a source of support, especially those faculty members who had a tie to the military themselves (e.g., a relative in the military) (Rumann, 2010). However, some faculty members may seem less than supportive (DiRamio et al., 2008; Persky & Oliver, 2010) and in some instances disrespectful based on the antiwar comments they make in class (Persky & Oliver, 2010). Student veterans may perceive others' negative feelings toward the wars in Iraq and Afghanistan as antimilitary, which may lead to feeling unwelcome on campus and in the classroom (Persky & Oliver, 2010). As a result of these differences, student veterans may feel marginalized not only by classmates but by faculty as well (Persky and Oliver, 2010).

Student veterans also experience the additional difficulty of navigating institutional bureaucracy and are sent from office to office when attempting to gather information related to GI Bill funding. Often, the student affairs professional responsible for helping student veterans navigate this process is the certifying official, whose primary responsibility is to serve as a liaison between the student and the Department of Veterans Affairs. However, these professionals often serve multiple roles for student veterans above and beyond their typical duties of certifying student veterans' enrollment at their institutions. Rumann (2010) found that many of the participants in his study identified the certifying official as the primary individual they looked to for support during their transition reenrolling into college and not simply as the person certifying their enrollment at the institution. Many institutions claim to be "veteran friendly," but if student veterans continue to encounter institutional bureaucracy and the lack of a concerted effort on the part of *all* community college faculty and staff to help ease their transitions, they will feel as though they do not matter.

Conclusions and Recommendations

Community colleges are well positioned to recruit and attract student veterans. Community colleges are also geared toward serving a nontraditional student population, which may make them an attractive alternative to student veterans who are trying to transition back into the civilian world following military service. Many community colleges are implementing initiatives to support this student population. Courses and orientation programs designed for student veterans and student veteran centers are steps in the right direction. However, that does not automatically mean community colleges are fully prepared to support this unique student population.

Student veterans attending community colleges may feel as though they are on the fringes of the campus community. They tend to feel different than most of the other students on campus and out of place as they transition from the military environment to the college environment. Without appropriate support and services, student veterans will likely feel disconnected from most of their college student peers, faculty, staff, and the campus community as a whole. Student veterans also are often not recognized outside of Veterans Day activities. Consequently, they often do not have a voice and tend not to be approached, despite having much to offer the campus community.

It is critical that community colleges take intentional steps to help support student veterans through policies, programs, strategies, and services. To help community college personnel do that, the authors offer the following recommendations and suggestions for action:

Campus-wide training for faculty, staff, and students to raise awareness of issues student veterans might face in college should be initiated (e.g., campus-wide forums designed to discuss student veterans' issues and concerns). Raising awareness is critical so that the responsibility of addressing student veterans' needs is not left up to one staff member or a handful of faculty members who have ties to the military.

Proactive efforts should include creating ways for student veterans to connect and interact with other veterans on campus. Creating student veteran organizations (e.g., SVA) is one way this could be addressed, but it is an area in which community colleges may be lagging behind. Establishing offices dedicated to student veterans is an excellent way to actively support student veterans on campus. Partnerships can also be established with community organizations (e.g., Veterans of Foreign Wars) to plan and implement programs and services that will best serve student veterans in college. Opportunities should also be provided to help student veterans connect with other nonmilitary members of the campus community, as misperceptions and misinformation may lead to student veterans feeling disconnected socially from others on campus.

Student veterans themselves should be consulted to help identify what needs to be done to effectively support student veterans on community college campuses. Too often, these students go unrecognized despite having much to offer other students, faculty, and staff at community colleges. As a rule, they possess strong leadership qualities and unique experiences and perspectives that could benefit the entire campus community. Rather than feeling silenced, student veterans' voices need to be heard.

References

Abrams, R. M. The U.S. military and higher education: A brief history. *Annals of the American Academy of Political and Social Science,* 1989, *502,* 15–28.

Bauman, M. C. *Called to serve: The military mobilization of undergraduates* (unpublished doctoral dissertation). University Park, PA: Pennsylvania State University, 2009.

Brint, S., & Karabel, J. The diverted dream: Community colleges and the promise of educational opportunity in America, 1900–1985. New York, NY: Oxford University Press, 1989.

Chappell, C. Veterans finding comfort on campus. *Community College Times,* 2010. Retrieved from www.communitycollegetimes.com/article.cfm?ArticleId=2724.

Cook, B. J., & Kim, Y. *From soldier to student: Easing the transition of service members on campus,* 2009. Retrieved from the American Council on Education web site: www.acenet.edu/AM/Template.cfm?Section=HENA&Template=/CM/ContentDisplay .cfm&ContentID=33233.

DiRamio, D., Ackerman, R., & Mitchell, R. L. From combat to campus: Voices of student-veterans. *NASPA Journal,* 2008, *45*(1), 73–102.

Eckstein, M. Colleges cite inequities in new benefits for veterans. *Chronicle of Higher Education,* 2009. Retrieved from http://chronicle.com/section/Home/5.

Ford, D., Northrup, P., & Wiley, L. Connections, partnerships, opportunities, and programs to enhance success for military students. In R. Ackerman & D. DiRamio (Eds.), *Creating a veteran-friendly campus: Strategies for transition and success. New Directions for Student Services,* No. 126 (pp. 61–69). San Francisco, CA: Jossey-Bass, 2009.

Katznelson, I. When affirmative action was white: An untold history of racial inequality in twentieth-century America. New York, NY: W. W. Norton, 2005.

Moltz, D. Anticipating impact of new GI Bill. *Inside Higher Ed,* 2009. Retrieved from www.insidehighered.com/.

Neiberg, M. S. Making citizen-soldiers: ROTC and the ideology of American military service, 2000. Cambridge, MA: Harvard University Press.

New York State Division of Veterans Affairs. *Education benefits,* 2010. Retrieved from http://veterans.ny.gov/education.html.

Olson, K. W. The G. I. Bill and higher education: Success and surprise. *American Quarterly,* 1973, *25*(5), 596–610.

Olson, K. W. *The G.I. Bill, the veterans, and the colleges.* Lexington: University Press of Kentucky, 1974.

Persky, K. R., & Oliver, D. E. *Veterans coming home to the community college: Linking research to practice*, 2010. Paper presented at the annual meeting of the Council for the Study of Community Colleges, Seattle, WA.

Quillen-Armstrong, S. Course to help transition veterans into civilian life. *Community College Times*, 2007. Retrieved from www.communitycollegetimes.com/article.cfm?ArticleId=417&PF=Y"PF=Y.

Radford, A. W. *Military service members and veterans in higher education: What the new GI Bill may mean for postsecondary institutions*, 2009. Retrieved from American Council on Education web site: www.acenet.edu/Content/NavigationMenu/Programs Services/CPA/Publications/MilService.errata.pdf.

Redden, E. 700 colleges tied the yellow ribbon. *Inside Higher Ed, 2009*. Retrieved from www.insidehighered.com/.

Rumann, C. B. *Student veterans returning to a community college: Understanding their transitions* (unpublished doctoral dissertation), 2010. Ames: Iowa State University.

Rumann, C. B., & Hamrick, F. A. Student veterans in transition: Re-enrolling after war zone deployments. *Journal of Higher Education, 2010, 81(4),* 431–458.

Sargent, W. M., Jr. Helping veterans transition into academic life through the creation of a university veteran support group: So we can better serve those who served us, 2009. Retrieved from ERIC database (ED 505889).

Servicemembers Opportunity Colleges. SOC consortium member institutions 2009–2011, 2011. Retrieved from www.soc.aascu.org/.

Sewall, M. Veterans use benefits of new GI Bill largely at for-profit and two-year colleges. *Chronicle of Higher Education*, 2010. Retrieved from www.chronicle.com.

Student Veterans of America *Student veterans establish national coalition*, 2008. Retrieved from www.studentveterans.org/media.html.

United States Department of Veterans Affairs. *Welcome to the GI Bill website: Education benefits*, 2009a. Retrieved from www.gibill.va.gov/GI_Bill_Info/benefits.htm.

United States Department of Veterans Affairs. *What is the Post 9/11 GI Bill?*, 2009b. Retrieved from www.gibill.va.gov/GI_Bill_Info/CH33/Post-911.htm.

University System of Ohio. *Ohio GI promise: Ohio's state level initiative.*, n.d. Retrieved from www.uso.edu/opportunities/ohioGIpromise/index.php.

COREY RUMANN *is an assistant professor and director of the College Student Affairs Program at the University of West Georgia in Carrollton, Georgia.*

MARISA RIVERA *is a lecturer and program coordinator in the Department of Education Leadership and Policy Studies at Iowa State University in Ames, Iowa.*

IGNACIO HERNANDEZ *is a doctoral student and research associate in the Community College Leadership Program at Iowa State University.*

NEW DIRECTIONS FOR COMMUNITY COLLEGES • DOI: 10.1002/cc

6

This chapter questions the dichotomous labeling and conceptualization of remedial and nonremedial students, particularly the added distinctions emphasized between four-year and two-year colleges, and it calls for a focus on the common challenges among all underprepared college students.

Beyond Remedial Dichotomies: Are 'Underprepared' College Students a Marginalized Marjority?

Regina Deil-Amen

With a majority of beginning community college students enrolling in remedial/developmental coursework, serving these once marginal students is now a central function of most community colleges. Approximately 60 percent of community college students entering college demonstrate a need for at least one remedial/developmental course (Adelman, 1996; Attewell, Lavin, Domina, and Levey, 2006), and some community colleges that serve mainly low-income and minority students now enroll a student population of which upwards of three-quarters need remediation (McClenney, 2009). Despite moving *numerically* from margin to center, these students are still *academically* marginalized in key ways by institutional designations. They exist in an ambiguous status in that they must pay for their enrollment in college courses and are allocated the privilege of financial aid and tend to define themselves as college students, yet their institutionally designated remedial status restricts their access to other college-level coursework and to the accumulation of some postsecondary degree credits. Therefore, their trajectories toward a postsecondary credential may be obscured and delayed institutionally based on these ambiguous definitions (Deil-Amen and Rosenbaum, 2002).

Rather than exploring the institutional dynamics relevant to the college pathways of underprepared students, such as those noted above, a good deal of research on the impact or effectiveness of remediation has instead focused on a comparison of the outcomes of remedial students with comparable samples of nonremedial students to argue the relative benefits or disadvantages of participation in remedial coursework (Attewell and and others, 2006; Bailey, 2009; Bettinger and Long, 2009; Calcagno and Long,

New Directions for Community Colleges, no. 155, Fall 2011 © 2011 Wiley Periodicals, Inc.
Published online in Wiley Online Library (wileyonlinelibrary.com) • DOI: 10.1002/cc.458

2008). Such studies have used complex and precise statistical tools and quasi-experimental approaches to account for selection bias and differences in the placement of students into remedial coursework, essentially creating opportunities to compare similarly prepared students exposed to different remedial "treatments." These important studies have shown mixed effects of remedial education. There are some modest positive results, but no strong evidence that access to remedial education in community college substantially facilitates or hinders credit or degree completion.

However, remedial students may have more in common with nonremedial students than one would presume from what has been highlighted in prior research. An overlooked finding of most prior studies of this topic (including those noted above) is that nearly all underprepared students—both those who are enrolled in remedial/developmental classes and those who are not—struggle to persist, and those in both categories who do persist are significantly delayed in their acquisition of a college credential. Fundamentally, such research has reinforced a well-known fact: being underprepared for college puts students at risk of noncompletion. This is apparently true regardless of whether or not students participate in remedial coursework, but the preceding studies fail to foreground this reality. In other words, the difference in college completion between students who demonstrate some measured lack of adequate preparation and those who do not is much greater than the difference between those enrolled and not enrolled in remediation.

Practices and policies should perhaps be aimed at dismantling old remedial-focused dichotomies in favor of a broader approach that encompasses the common challenges faced by all underprepared students, regardless of their institutional label/designation as remedial or non-remedial. The work of two leading scholars supports such a refocus from narrowly construed dichotomous definitions toward a broader approach. Clifford Adelman (1999, 2006), in exploring the pathways of students pursuing four-year degrees, highlights the prominence of high school academic rigor over remedial placement in influencing bachelor's degree completion. Thomas Bailey (2009) offers suggestions and insights based on data regarding community college students, and he emphasizes the fact that "two-thirds or more of community college students enter college with academic skills weak enough in at least one major subject area to threaten their ability to succeed in college-level courses" (p. 13).

Definitions of and Variation Within and Outside the Remedial Student Status

Ambiguity surrounds institutional definitions of which students are designated with remedial status. Within community colleges, remedial/developmental status is most often defined as a result of students' placement testing in any of three areas—reading, writing (or English), and math.

NEW DIRECTIONS FOR COMMUNITY COLLEGES • DOI: 10.1002/cc

Students who score below a particular level of college competence are rec-ommended for placement into below-college-level classes. However, as sev-eral researchers have documented, substantial variation exists both within and across states, districts, and institutions in terms of how students get placed and which students get placed into remedial-level coursework. In some states, such as Ohio, placement into remedial coursework differs between institutions (Bettinger and Long, 2005), while in Florida, a com-mon placement test score determines placement statewide (Calcagno and Long, 2008).

For states without the systematic policies that Florida has enacted, variation between districts and institutions can be extensive. Some districts make enrollment in the remedial class mandatory, while others allow the student to choose whether or not they will enroll at the level into which they tested. Some individual community colleges make remedial courses mandatory based on placement test scores, while other community colleges within the same district relegate the task of actual enrollment into these classes to counselors and advisors who recommend and encourage such remedial class enrollment (Levin and Calcagno, 2008). Furthermore, in six states, Perin (2006) finds community colleges often mandate student assessment for remedial course placement and then require that low-scoring students enroll in remedial courses even when the states do not mandate it. She also finds that faculty and instructors even routinely over-ride mandatory assessment and placement policies so that students can bypass remedial classes, and some students avoid testing altogether. The types of instruments used for assessment varied tremendously, with addi-tional subjective measures, including the institution's own tests, course grades, and student self-reports, influencing placement decisions. In addi-tion, practices used to determine student readiness to advance in or exit from remediation vary widely (Perin, 2006). I found similar practices in my own research in Illinois, where placement practices differed even within a multicampus district. Students with the same placement test results routinely placed into remedial classes at one campus location and higher-level classes at another campus location. Overall, within the remedial/developmental category, there is quite a bit of variation in the levels of preparation and course-taking patterns that exist across states, districts, and institutions.

In light of this variation, it is not surprising that there are striking simi-larities between students designated as remedial/developmental and those not designated as such *within* community colleges as well as among remedial students *across* the two-year and four-year college divide. As noted above, a slippery slope characterizes the placement and classification systems that determine who enrolls in remedial courses and who does not. In fact, Calcagno and Long (2008), using a regression discontinuity approach, claim that enough similarity exists between students above and below the "cutoff" placement score that such a distinction can be considered arbitrary, and few differences exist in the short- and long-term trajectories of these students. Other work reveals that remedial students enrolled in nonselective universities in Ohio face challenges perhaps as extreme as remedial students who populate the state's community colleges (Bettinger and Long, 2004). Despite these similarities between remedial and nonremedial students and between underprepared students across institution types, scholars and institutions use language, policy, and practice to marginalize remedial students and community college students relative to other students who are essentially at a very similar level of achievement. This puts community college remedial students at risk of being doubly marginalized.

Ambiguity at the Margins

Ironically, such language and practices also create ambiguity of definition, which conceals these formal status distinctions from external scrutiny. Most remedial math and reading or writing courses are college credit bearing and qualify for financial aid—making them distinct from "noncredit" classes—even though many of these remedial classes cannot be applied for the purposes of transfer and some degree options. In this way, community colleges appear to be offering more "college"-level classes than they actually are offering, and student financial aid dollars are applied to this set of conditions. Related issues are reflected in the work of Deil-Amen and Rosenbaum (2002), who found remedial coursework in a sample of two-year colleges in the Midwest to be labeled in a way that obscured the classes' remedial status, thus confusing students who did not realize these classes would extend their timetable to degree completion and would not count toward their degree requirements. Remedial classes were not clearly designated as distinct from similarly labeled classes in the same subject.

Such research in a Midwestern city was conducted a decade ago, yet a decade later in a district in another state in the Southwest, the same ambiguous labeling and lack of clarity continues. For example, the language used to describe math offerings at Pima Community College in Arizona includes no indication of remedial, developmental, or below college level (https://bannerweb.pima.edu/pls/pima/az_tw_zipsched.p_search). In fact, three levels of math can be applied toward an associate's degree but not toward transfer, and this is not clearly indicated either. Whereas the English Composition/Writing requirements are less ambiguous, with Writing 101 serving as the first level of such class credit for both associate's degrees and transfer credit. However, only some of the classes below the 101 level are labeled as "developmental" while others, including WRT 100, are not, yet they clearly are remedial in that they do not count as credit toward any degree or transfer pathways.

Adding to the complexity is the possibly growing trend of universities to "outsource" to community colleges the instruction of their below-college-level classes. When the idea of four-year colleges passing the responsibility for remediation on to community colleges is discussed, we typically think of how institutions like the City University of New York (CUNY) might refuse to admit students who score below a placement threshold that identifies them as needing remedial coursework. However, under revenue pressures, a growing number of broader access universities may still be enrolling "remedial" students despite state-level and other policies. For instance, Arizona universities have been engaging in arrangements with local community colleges to allow admitted university students to take one or more below-college-level classes at the community college while paying tuition and receiving financial aid as university students.

Despite these developments, absent from the research literature is an acknowledgment that students who gain admission to nonselective or moderately selective universities are also marginal. Students at the University of Arizona, for instance, can be admitted with up to three "deficiencies." Therefore, although state policies in many states, including Arizona, "prohibit public four-year universities from offering remedial education" (Bettinger and Long, 2005, p. 17), throughout the past decade, Arizona universities do not prevent their "deficient" admits from taking one or two community college remedial classes until they are ready to place into college-level classes. This practice may be more widespread than researchers realize. In fact, at the University of Arizona, typically, placement test results place more than a third of the incoming freshman class below the lowest level of math offered at the university and therefore enrolls students in any one of four levels of lower-level math at Pima Community College (PCC). Interestingly, the proportion of freshmen at the university enrolled in the community college's remedial classes in any given semester is not much lower than the proportion of PCC enrollments in such math classes overall—approximately 40 percent at the downtown campus.

The ambiguity in the definition of remedial status previously noted is further complicated by such intersections and fluid boundaries exemplified by these "remedial" class enrollments of four-year college students in community colleges. In the example of the University of Arizona, the lowest level of math at the university has traditionally been Math 112, but at PCC, in which students enroll if they place below Math 112, the classes include Math 122 and lower numbers. So the potential for confusion abounds since Pima's Math 122 is actually a lower-level math than the university's Math 112, and "college"-level math at Pima begins with Math 142.

Another example of university student marginality is the fact that many university students enroll in and then subsequently fail college-level classes. Again, this is more typical for math and science classes. These students then have to retake these classes again, and they either do so at the university or at their local community college while still enrolled as university students. Such examples blur the lines between who is a remedial student and who is not and foreground the delays and challenges of students who are not officially designated as remedial students, but who face significant danger of nonpersistence due to failing nonremedial classes for which they are not prepared. Few studies have examined the ramifications of dropped and failed classes among community college and four-year college students who are not of remedial status. These students constitute a potentially marginalized and certainly at-risk population who are overlooked due to our focus on categorizing and contrasting along the remedial/nonremedial and the two-year/four-year divides. Such students do not initially place into remediation, but they are clearly at risk of noncompletion. Recent research on patterns of enrollment at multiple institutions and increases in reverse transfer, particularly among low-socioeconomic-status students, lend more evidence to this growing segment of the undergraduate population (Goldrick-Rab, 2006; Goldrick-Rab and Pfeffer, 2009).

Experiences of Students at the Margins of the University

In my current research, hundreds of students who participate in summer bridge programs and income-based scholarship programs at the University of Arizona were interviewed as part of two separate studies. Many of these university students experienced some form of enrollment in classes at Pima Community College. These students fell into three groups. One group took Pima classes in their first semester based on their placement test scores. This was the group most likely to be enrolled in a remedial-level class. Another group took Pima classes in their second semester after dropping or receiving a D or lower in a math or English class during their first semester at the university. A third group took classes in the summer following their first year or in their sophomore year, after they received a grade point average low enough to put them on academic probation at the university. The vast majority of the students interviewed for this study were underrepresented racial minority students. Interestingly, these students were quite different from underrepresented students I had interviewed in my research in Chicago (Deil-Amen and Rosenbaum, 2002; Rosenbaum, Deil-Amen, and Person, 2006). In that prior research, students showed little evidence of feeling stigmatized by their remedial or underprepared status, or their movement as reverse transfers from four-year to two-year colleges (Deil-Amen and Goldrick-Rab, 2009). In contrast, in my current research, the university students seem to be greatly affected by a fear of being stigmatized, and they experience stereotype threat as well, often fearing that they will be the example of the low-achieving minority student that their peers and instructors expect.

While those students—especially those racial minority students—who gain access to universities are often viewed as the success stories relative to those who enroll in community colleges, my research reveals that these students are similarly vulnerable to failure, particularly if they find themselves underprepared to succeed at the university. Below, the perspectives

NEW DIRECTIONS FOR COMMUNITY COLLEGES • DOI: 10.1002/cc

and challenges of specific students who found themselves enrolled in community college classes at some point are highlighted as examples of the larger trends. Some of the huge lecture classes at the university present these students with additional challenges that community college students rarely face. As Selena explained, "Well, about the classes, it is like it is so big. I mean some classes are over 100 students and that stresses me out. I cannot concentrate. I did not expect that. I expected regular classes like 30 people. I mean those are the classes I have been having a little more trouble with."

Over three quarters of the students interviewed experienced a serious academic challenge upon enrollment, and nearly a quarter of students resisted seeking help because they feared that they were too incompetent to belong in college or that others would perceive them to be incompetent as college students. Ayanna is a good example of a student who struggled in her large lecture class but did not go to the professor for "extra help" because she attached a "bad stigma" to getting extra assistance. She felt, "I should be able to do this on my own." Chandra admitted, ". . . at first I thought that if everyone around me is getting this, why aren't I getting it, too, and I kind of thought there was something wrong with my head. . . . at first I'm just thinking I don't know if this is for me. I don't understand any of this, and it made me feel bad for a while because I'm like is it just me or is it because of the way I grew up?" Mark's comments reveal how gender also played into students' negative views on needing additional help to succeed in college. He did not seek much assistance in his first semester, was on academic probation in his second semester, and said, "I really probably should look for, like, more help, but I haven't really. I've been an independent person for a while and I'm trying to keep that going. . . . My motto is to be a man you need to learn how to survive all by yourself."

Students' fears of being exposed as inadequate were compounded by their lack of feelings of entitlement. They expressed feeling that they would be imposing on college professors and staff by requesting guidance and help. Carlos expressed this sentiment:

> Yeah sometimes I had real difficulties trying to get a subject in the class, and people were there to help me. I could have easily just gone to office hours or something and I just decided to stick to myself and try to do it myself, and it didn't end up so well because I didn't really get the grasp of the subject. And then I would have to go into class and have a test or a quiz so it didn't really work out that well. . . . I think I did that because I felt going and asking for much help was taking their time and bothering them so much I guess. And now I know that's what they are there for and I have to take advantage of them because they are there to help.

This qualitative research reveals portions of the social-psychological perspectives that inform the decisions and behaviors of university students who find themselves facing steep academic challenges and enrolled in "remedial" community classes despite their admission to a selective university.

What Works and Doesn't Work: Recent Remedial Interventions and Their Impact

Prior evaluations of remedial student learning outcomes have looked within institutions and within specific classrooms to determine what pedagogical approaches appear to work best to improve the learning of remedial students (Boylan, 2002; Levin and Koski, 1998). Much of this research, however, is descriptive or documents correlational relationships, and it is not designed to identify potential causal relationships between the interventions and remedial student outcomes. More recently, longitudinal evaluations of interventions at multiple institutions using random assignment provide more rigorous tests of what approaches yield desired results. Perin and Hare (2010) conducted research using randomized controls to test the effectiveness of particular interventions on the skill acquisition of remedial/developmental reading students at three community colleges. Preliminary results show reading and writing skills improvement for the students participating in this Content Comprehensive Strategy Intervention (CCSI), which combines practice in critical reading and writing skills with additional academic support and a focus on engaging students in reading passages specific to students' interests—anatomy and physiology for some groups and more generic high-interest themes for others. The control group did not receive the interventions. Another project involves six community colleges participating in the National Center for Postsecondary Research's Learning Communities Demonstration. Researchers are attempting to determine if learning communities are an effective strategy for helping students who need developmental education. Thus far, findings from one of the community colleges in Florida reveal no meaningful impact on students' academic success for the full study sample. However, evidence shows positive impacts on some educational outcomes for the third cohort of students, suggesting a honing and maturing of the program may have resulted in improvements relevant to the desired outcomes. In particular, faculty collaboration and curricular integration may have finally led to some increases in student academic success (Weiss, Visher, and Wathington, 2010).

Conclusion

The content of this chapter has attempted to broaden the discussion of remediation in key ways by moving beyond a discussion of community college remedial students to address the larger population of two-year and four-year students who begin college at the margins of "college-level" readiness. In creating an artificial dividing line between remedial and nonremedial students, the broad scope of the issue of underpreparedness becomes truncated, and debates become narrowly focused on differences between remedial and nonremedial course taking, and the context of these debates narrowly focuses on community colleges rather than including broad access universities that are also enrolling huge populations of underprepared students (Venezia and Kirst, 2005).

Similarities, differences, and overlap exist between two and four-year underprepared students and should be acknowledged and incorporated into research and programmatic agendas. In particular, it should be recognized that the key issue of concern is that a majority of underprepared community college enrollees—both those who are enrolled in remedial coursework and those who are not—fail to persist at very high rates. The research on the impact of specific interventions with remedial/developmental students is a step in the right direction to determine what works with this population. However, the work of practitioners like Professor Peter Adams at the Community College of Baltimore County should be examined carefully as well. He has advocated for and created an approach to developmental writing that mainstreams these students with college-level students and accelerates their learning through the provision of extra support through an additional shadow class offering extra advising and skill-building. His own internal tracking of outcomes demonstrates major increases in retention and progress to the next level (Adams, 2010). This applied research he has been engaging in at his own institution provides some food for thought. His interventions break the traditional dichotomy of remedial/nonremedial by teaching remedial students in the same classroom alongside students who placed into college-level English. Perhaps the success of such local strategies can inform more broadly applied and evaluated interventions.

Given the massiveness of the underprepared majority and the extensive variation within it, the larger picture begs the following questions for future research:

1. How can we move beyond a discussion of community college remedial students to better define the larger population of two-year and four-year students who begin college at the margins of "college-level" readiness?
2. How can we begin to understand the similarities, differences, and overlap between two and four-year underprepared students?
3. How and why do the majority of underprepared community college enrollees (both those who are enrolled in remedial coursework and those who are not) fail to persist at such high rates?
4. For those who do persist and are not enrolled in remedial coursework, why are so many proceeding just as slowly toward degree completion as those enrolled in remedial coursework? Essentially, what practices and behaviors are delaying those underprepared students who are not enrolling in remedial courses?

NEW DIRECTIONS FOR COMMUNITY COLLEGES • DOI: 10.1002/cc

In terms of policy and practice, efforts need to both account for variations within the developmental population and extend across false dichotomies that categorize and thereby marginalize students by remedial/developmental status or institution of enrollment.

Recommendations for Action.   Research and practice at both community colleges and broad access universities may benefit from a shift away from the tendency to create dichotomies between remedial and nonremedial students and between community college and four-year college student populations. First, with so much research focused on disentangling the impact of remedial participation on various persistence and completion outcomes, too little attention has been paid to figuring out what works to improve learning *and* persistence for any student who is underprepared. Until very recently, a focus on learning has been completely divorced from a focus on longer-term persistence and degree acquisition outcomes. Evaluations of remedial/developmental approaches continue to yield little evidence of the effectiveness of remedial approaches relative to other approaches or the effectiveness of particular remedial/developmental interventions. Future research should work in collaboration with community colleges and instructors to simultaneously assess the effect of interventions on both learning and longer-term persistence and completion outcomes for underprepared students.

Such research should not be limited to what happens within particular classrooms. As Perin (2005) describes, community colleges differ widely in their organizational and instructional approaches to developmental education, and these variations need to be considered when decisions are made about trying to improve learning and other outcomes for remedial and other underprepared students, particularly in the context of changing demographics. It is important to always consider that the delivery of educational services occurs within a larger institutional context and an even broader sociocultural and economic context that heavily influences student trajectories. How students interpret their learning and college participation within the larger context of their lives and identities and make decisions based on these complex dynamics is a key component too often neglected in educational research. The work described above and other recent research address the importance of students' decision-making processes and strategizing based on their social context (Cox, 2009; Deil-Amen and Tevis, 2010). By excluding these processes from research agendas, educational researchers are signaling their lack of attention to the sociological and psychological elements of all human interaction. Better understanding the larger social context and immediate social-psychological processes at work can help evaluators and researchers better interpret the short-term and long-term results of particular pedagogical approaches—for both remedial and other underprepared students who are not in remedial classes but facing similar challenges.

As an important component of such research, we should include how remedial programming and instruction is actually organized and implemented within institutions and among institutional leaders. Perin's prior work on this topic highlights the centrality of these organizational dynamics (Perin, 2002a, 2002b). Also, the study of learning community interventions noted above shows the dynamics of organizational implementation are pivotal, including the need for consensus about the standards for college-level work, faculty collaboration, curricular integration, administrator support, and an alignment between assessment for placement and diagnosis for instruction (Safran and Visher, 2010). A research agenda that includes the four elements of (1) student learning, (2) persistence and completion outcomes, (3) student strategizing and decision making, and (4) organizational implementation represents a more comprehensive approach that has not yet been brought to fruition.

Second, community colleges and scholars interested in research on these institutions should focus some attention on students who show evidence of being underprepared yet are not labeled as remedial status. These students may be caught in a cycle of dropping and/or failing classes early on in their college trajectory—a pattern that jeopardizes not only their learning, but also their cumulative grade point average and their chances of successful persistence and degree completion. At four-year colleges, underprepared students are also at risk in the same way and should receive enhanced advising, mentoring, and academic support. Longitudinal studies can track the course-taking patterns of these students to identify how and where students begin on a path toward withdrawal or failure. Students who are not officially classified as "remedial" but who are taking remedial classes at community colleges initially or after failing to pass college-level courses may be particularly at risk. Universities and community colleges should work in partnership around remedial/developmental education, particularly since "below college level" at the university is defined differently than at the community college. This situation, in which local community colleges may be teaching the students considered "remedial" by universities, deserves further attention. Overall, it is important for institutions and policy makers to question the practices and behaviors that are delaying so many students who are *not* enrolled in remedial coursework, causing them to proceed just as slowly toward degree completion as those enrolled in remedial coursework.

Finally, community colleges should work to create more transparency in the language used to convey which classes can and cannot be used toward associate degree requirements and which classes can and cannot be transferred for credit to a four-year college and for which majors. For researchers, it is less important to classify students as remedial or nonremedial, and more important to identify the college preparation opportunities and postenrollment interventions that best promote learning and persistence. It is less important to decipher if two-year beginners fare worse than four-year beginners in terms of BA completion than it is to identify subgroups of similarly underprepared two- and four-year beginners to determine how institutions can best respond to their unique experiences and challenges. Taken together, underprepared students—if defined across two-year and four-year institutions and across the remedial/nonremedial divide—likely constitute a majority of undergraduates. No longer can we continue to consider them as a problematic "other" in need of special programming. They now represent the norm in our higher education system.

References

Adams, P. Creative ways to deal with remedial/developmental education. Persistence in high school and college: Tools to increase persistence and degree attainment. Princeton University, 2010.

Adelman, C. The truth about remedial work: It's more complex than windy rhetoric and simple solutions suggest. *Chronicle of Higher Education,* 1996, A56.

Adelman, C. *Answers in the tool box: Academic intensity, attendance patterns, and bachelor's degree attainment.* Washington, DC: U.S. Dept. of Education, Office of Educational Research and Improvement, 1999.

Adelman, C. *The toolbox revisited: Paths to degree completion from high school through college.* Washington, DC: Office of Vocational and Adult Education, U.S. Dept. of Education, 2006.

Attewell, P., Lavin, D., Domina, T., and Levey, T. New Evidence on College Remediation. *Journal of Higher Education,* 2006, 77(5), 886–924.

Bailey, T. Challenge and opportunity: Rethinking the role and function of developmental education in community college [part of the special issue, Policies and Practices to Improve Student Preparation and Success]. *New Directions for Community Colleges,* 2009, No. 145, 11–30.

Bettinger, E., & Long, B. T. Addressing the needs of underprepared students in higher education: Does college remediation work? *Journal of Human Resources,* 2009, 44(3), 736–771.

Bettinger, E., and Long, B. T. Remediation at the community college: Student participation and outcomes. In C. A. Kozeracki (Ed.), *Responding to the challenges of developmental education. New Directions for Community Colleges, 129.* San Francisco, CA: Jossey-Bass, 2005.

Bettinger, E., and Long, B. T. *Shape up or ship out: The effects of remediation on students at four-year colleges.* NBER Working Paper 10369, National Bureau of Economic Research, Inc., 2004.

Boylan, H. *What works: A guide to research-based best practices in developmental education.* Boone, NC: Appalachian State University, Continuous Quality Improvement Network with the National Center for Developmental Education, 2002.

Calcagno, J. C., and Long, B. T. The impact of postsecondary remediation using a regression discontinuity approach: Addressing endogenous sorting and noncompliance. New York: National Center for Postsecondary Research, 2008.

Cox, R. D. Promoting success while addressing students' fear of failure. *Community College Review,* 37(10), 52–80, 2009.

Deil-Amen, R., & Goldrick-Rab, S. *Institutional transfer and the management of risk in higher education.* WISCAPE Working Paper, 2009.

Deil-Amen, R., and Rosenbaum, J. The unintended consequences of stigma-free remediation. *Sociology of Education,* 2002, 75(3), 249–268.

Deil-Amen, R., & Tevis, T. Circumscribed agency: The relevance of standardized college entrance exams for low SES high school students. *Review of Higher Education,* 2010, 33(2), 141–175.

Goldrick-Rab, S. Following their every move: An investigation of social class differences in college pathways. *Sociology of Education,* 2006, *79*(1), 61–79.

Goldrick-Rab, S., & Pfeffer, F. T. Beyond access: Explaining socioeconomic differences in college transfer. *Sociology of Education,* 2009, *82*(2), 101–125.

Levin, H., and Calcagno, J. C. Remediation in the community college: An evaluator's perspective. *Community College Review,* 2008, *35*(3), 181–207.

Levin, H., and Koski, W. Administrative approaches to educational productivity. In J. E. Groccia and J. E. Miller (Eds.), *Enhancing productivity: Administrative, instructional, and technological strategies. New Directions for Higher Education, 103,* 9–21. San Francisco, CA: Jossey-Bass, 1998.

McClenney, K. Helping community-college students succeed: A moral imperative. *Chronicle of Higher Education,* 2009, *55*(33), A60.

Perin, D. Curriculum and pedagogy for academic-occupational integration in community colleges: Illustrations from an instrumental case study—Parts I–IX. *Teachers College Record,* 2002a.

Perin, D. The location of developmental education in community colleges: A discussion of the merits of mainstreaming vs. centralization. *Community College Review,* 2002b, *30,* 27–44.

Perin, D. Institutional decision making for increasing academic preparedness in community colleges. *New Directions in Community Colleges: Responding to the Challenges of Developmental Education,* 2005, *129,* 27–38.

Perin, D. Can community colleges protect both access and standards? The problem of remediation. *Teachers College Record,* 2006, *108*(3), 339–373.

Perin, D., & Hare, R. *A contextualized reading-writing intervention for community college students* (CCRC Brief No. 44). New York: Community College Research Center, Teachers College, Columbia University, 2010.

Rosenbaum, J. E., Deil-Amen, R., and Person, A. E. *After admission: From college access to college success.* New York, NY: Russell Sage Foundation, 2006.

Safran, S., & Visher, M. G. Case studies of three community colleges: The policy and practice of assessing and placing students in developmental education courses. NCPR Working Paper, 2010.

Venezia, A., and Kirst, M. W. Inequitable opportunities: How current education systems and policies undermine the chances for student persistence and success in college. *Educational Policy,* 2005, *19*(2), 283–307.

Weiss, M. J., Visher, M. G., and Wathington, H. Learning communities for students in developmental reading: An impact study at Hillsborough Community College. (MDRC), NCPR Working Paper, 2010.

REGINA DEIL-AMEN is an associate professor in the Department of Educational Policy Studies and Practice and currently serves as director of the Center for the Study of Higher Education at the University of Arizona.

7

Part-time professors often feel marginal to the educational process of their schools, and this outsider status is exacerbated for those who teach college in prison.

Borderland Stories about Teaching College in Prison

Susanna Spaulding

If part-time faculty members in American community colleges are strangers in their own land (Roueche, Roueche, & Milliron, 1995), the metaphor of stranger applies even more poignantly to those part-time faculty who teach college in prison and become "strangers in a strange land" (Wright, 2006, p. 375). Going inside the prison to teach is similar to traveling to a foreign country and encountering a new culture. When educators enter the prison, they experience a physical and social distance from other groups such as teachers on the outside, prison system employees, community members, and even family. At the same time, this transition to an unfamiliar environment provides prison educators with intrinsic rewards such as opportunities for personal and professional growth.

Although educators who teach college in prison feel marginal in their interactions with higher education institutions and correctional systems, they feel central in their role as teachers where they matter in the lives of their inmate-students. Many prison educators are not full participants in the correctional system, and they are not full-time members of the higher education community. They are contracted on a part-time basis through local universities and, most frequently, through community colleges (Erisman & Contardo, 2005) to teach college courses in local correctional facilities.

My contribution to this exploration of marginalized populations in community colleges was a narrative inquiry into the lived experiences of five educators who taught college in prison (Spaulding, 2008). I was interested in how these educators negotiated the prison system, which is "the most restrictive environment for education" (Eggleston & Gehring, 2000, p. 306). The

NEW DIRECTIONS FOR COMMUNITY COLLEGES, no. 155, Fall 2011 © 2011 Wiley Periodicals, Inc.
Published online in Wiley Online Library (wileyonlinelibrary.com) • DOI: 10.1002/cc.459

participants in my study had not planned a career in prison education, and once they had an opportunity, they persisted because teaching college courses in prison was mainly a positive experience with personal and professional rewards. In addition, they realized that their instruction offered the potential for intellectual growth in their inmate-students. Some insight into the experiences of feeling marginal and feeling central may result from exploring what drives these educators to work in an environment that places the priority on security and social control rather than on education's goals of self-directed learning and free exchange of ideas.

In order to situate the stories these educators told about teaching college in prison, I begin this chapter with a brief overview of prison education in the United States. Next, I present the themes that emerged from my narrative inquiry into the experiences of the prison educators with whom I spoke. Their stories centered on working in a borderland, negotiating power relations, and making personal transformations. Then I offer two conceptual frameworks that are useful in understanding the experience of teaching college in prison. Finally, I recommend that community colleges expand their involvement in prison education by describing several successful collaborations among community colleges, universities, nonprofit organizations, and state corrections systems to provide access to higher education for prisoners.

An Overview of College Programs in Prisons

Throughout the history of prison higher education in the United States, a tension has existed between the importance of security that ensures the confinement of society's deviants and the value of treatment that seeks to promote changes in the behavior of incarcerated individuals. Consequently, public support for correctional programming has vacillated between the two opposing approaches of punishment and reform. Furthermore, these changes in public opinion about the meanings of incarceration and the perceptions of the criminal have shaped the strategies for prison education (Silva, 1994).

Historical Context of Prison Education.   Some type of education has existed in American prisons throughout their over 200-year history. The first prison keepers were Quakers in post-Revolutionary Philadelphia, who believed that restorative rather than punitive programs were more effective in returning offenders to society. In this approach, known as the Pennsylvania System, prisoners were kept in total isolation, treated humanely, and provided with rudimentary moral education. In contrast, the Auburn System emerged in the early 1890s in New York State and established mass production industries where the prisoners worked together during the day in monotonous routine tasks. Proponents of the Auburn System held that "educational efforts in prisons were unwise because they took time away from the inmates' labor" (Silva, 1994, p. 20).

NEW DIRECTIONS FOR COMMUNITY COLLEGES • DOI: 10.1002/cc

By the last half of the 19th century, a more complex notion of the criminal had emerged. At the Elmira Reformatory in New York, a penal philosophy was implemented in which "society bore at least some of the burden for the miscreant's behavior" (Silva, 1994, p. 21). In this approach, criminals were considered products of their environment and economic status and should be allowed an opportunity for regeneration. This penal philosophy started the Reformatory era, which included job-specific education and the first postsecondary education programs.

20th-Century Approach to Prison Education.   At the beginning of the 20th century, American society identified a need for universal secondary education while prisons recognized the utility of vocational education. Accordingly, the prisons implemented correspondence courses in vocational and remedial academic areas. In 1923, Columbia University offered college-level correspondence courses to inmates at Sing Sing Prison from the viewpoint that academic courses gave inmates an incentive to improve their lives. During this period, some universities also offered college courses in the prisons. However, the Great Depression reduced interest in prison education, and the general public reverted to the Auburn System of prison policy, which focused on prison labor.

After World War II, the benefits of the GI Bill brought thousands of veterans to university campuses. This influx of older students forced universities to consider the phenomenon of adult education, and the resultant expansion of access to the college degree included higher education for incarcerated learners. In 1953, Southern Illinois University at Carbondale implemented the first degree program in an Illinois State prison funded by state aid and university grants. Since funding was a persistent problem, the growth of prison education programs was slow. Ten years after the first college degree program in prison was established, state and federal prisons housed only a dozen postsecondary programs.

In 1965, Congress passed Title IV of the Higher Education Act, which was the "single most important event in the development of higher education for prisoners (and other low-income students, for that matter)" (Silva, 1994, p. 26). A major part of Title IV was the need-based Basic Education Opportunity Grants, which later were named "Pell Grants," in honor of Rhode Island Senator Claiborne Pell, who sponsored the bill. Since prisoners usually qualified for the Pell Grant program because of their minimum income, prison college programs entered a stage of rapid expansion. From 1968 to 1982, the number of prison college programs grew from approximately 15 to 350 programs and were offered in the majority of states.

This progressive trend was reversed by the early 1990s with an increase in prison construction, mandatory sentencing, and the exclusion of inmates from entitlement education programs. According to Edwards (1993), the prison system in the United States became "our country's principal government program for the poor" (p. 316). At the time of their arrest, most state prison inmates were jobless or holding only part-time jobs, and did not have a high school degree or equivalent. As of 1986, inmates in state prisons had earned less than $10,000 annually a year before incarceration.

From 1982 through 1994, conservative politicians in Washington, D.C., introduced bills annually to curtail Pell Grants for incarcerated learners. Finally, the passage of the 1994 Violent Crime Control Act, which President Clinton signed, eliminated all state and federal inmates' eligibility for Pell entitlement grants effective in the 1995–1996 academic year. Before this legislation, 92 percent of correctional systems offered some form of postsecondary education and this percentage was reduced to 63 percent by 1995 (Tewksbury, Erickson, & Taylor, 2000). The elimination of Pell Grants for inmate education resulted in a decrease of enrollment in postsecondary correction education programs from 38,000 to 21,000 and significantly decreased curriculum diversity.

Prison Education in the Post–Pell Grant Era.   More recent studies found that the number of college programs in prison has not decreased as much as many researchers and educators had predicted. Many college-level correctional education programs now receive funding from the federal Incarcerated Youthful Offender (IYO) grants that Congress approved in 2002. At their inception, these grants stipulated that subsidized students must be offenders who are 25 years old or younger and are within five years of release from prison. Older inmates may enroll in the college programs by paying the college tuition. All inmate-students must pass the General Education Development (GED) tests or have a high school diploma to participate in these college courses, which are frequently core general education courses. The state's department of corrections uses federal funding or state appropriations for contracts with a local community college or university that provides the curriculum and instructors for these college-level correctional education programs.

The Prison Educator Experience

For my narrative study, I interviewed five educators who had taught college courses in a western state's youth and adult correctional facilities contracted through several local community colleges and one university. In a series of in-depth and unstructured interviews, each participant told stories that reflected differing perspectives of her or his role as a prison educator. They exercised individual strategies for resolving the tension between the prison administration's focus on inmate control and the educator's desire to create a classroom with open dialogue and discussion among the inmate-students. Although they were distinctive in their motivation, education, length of time teaching college in prison, and prior work experience, my study participants shared a passion for teaching and had mainly positive experiences with their inmate-students.

These educators entered the prison system to teach college courses as "outsiders" who were unfamiliar with the prison's unique culture. Using

NEW DIRECTIONS FOR COMMUNITY COLLEGES • DOI: 10.1002/cc

pseudonyms during the interviews, the educators talked about coming to the decision to teach in prison, feeling fear or frustration with the ambiguity of the task, experiencing the physical and emotional environment of the prison, and adjusting personal opinions of incarceration and of their inmate-students. Their stories reflected marginalization and isolation, complicity with and the countering of the prison hierarchical power structure, and tolerance of and alignment with the Other: that is, the prisoner. From clusters of these descriptions, three central themes emerged that I identified as working in borderlands, negotiating power relations, and making personal transformations.

Working in Borderlands. In the interviews, these educators described their feelings of isolation, dislocation, and dissonance when teaching college in prison. They were distanced from other groups on the inside including full-time correctional teaching staff, inmates, and correctional officers. On the outside, even their friends, family, and colleagues were unable to relate to this experience of going inside the prison walls. When these educators went into the prison for the first time, they experienced the shock of facing surroundings very different from those to which they were accustomed. One of their first startling experiences was entering the main part of the prison through the security gates, which close in front and behind the visitor for a security check. As Seldom (a pseudonym) explained, "When that [iron gate] slams shut, you realize that you're enclosed. That's why they call it the trap."

As the community college educators tried to negotiate the dynamics of the prison system, they often became frustrated. For example, Gandalf (a pseudonym) described conducting a class when she was interrupted by a message on the prison loud speaker that she did not understand. However, her students immediately packed up their books and said, "We gotta go now." This is consistent with research by Weiss and Fine (2004), who found that outsiders are disadvantaged because they misunderstand the "tightly woven fabrics of organizational life" (p. 111) in prison. In an attempt to make meaning, outsiders try to break the prison culture down into discrete elements. However, insiders, such as inmates and correctional officials, understand how the discrete features of the prison community are deeply connected. These insiders also understand the dynamics of the dominant discourse of power and the counter narrative of vulnerability and resistance or compliance.

Negotiating Power Relations.   Within the prison, the role of teachers is to provide a place where inmate-students can gather and talk among themselves (Linebaugh, 1995). The classroom becomes a space like the laundry room, the kitchen, or the yard, where the inmates have private discussions before returning to their cells. However, these educators had limited resources to create an atmosphere of learning since they were hired by the community college and not by the prison system, which focused on security rather than education. For example, Ulysses (a pseudonym) conducted an evening class in the prison's visiting room, which was loud and dirty, without standard classroom supplies and furniture. Still, he seemed to create a space of trust and respect that was free of fear or danger so that his inmate-students could feel safe and focus on studying. Furthermore, Ulysses talked about the respect that he had and demonstrated for his inmate-students.

Another aspect of negotiating power relations within the prison culture is exemplified when these educators adjusted to their new surroundings and created a type of hybrid pedagogy to meet the unique and practical education needs of their inmate-students. They learned to develop new methods for teaching that worked in prisons within the hierarchical power structure. Jack (a pseudonym) offered an example of adapting to and resisting the prison environment. He was teaching chemistry and wanted to demonstrate a certain characteristic of the topic they were learning. He brought some harmless props into the prison without explaining to the correctional officers that he was going to use them in an experiment to illustrate the principle of combustion. He said, "They [corrections officers] had no idea. I knew they wouldn't go for that, so I just did it. Sub rosa."

In some ways, the participants felt empowered within their prison classrooms to structure curricula that met the needs of their inmate-students and fit with their personal values. As another example, Kathryn (a pseudonym) used her philosophy and ethics courses to help the students begin to take personal responsibility for violating the legal rights of other members of society. Through a dialogic and democratic classroom that promoted transformative learning, she helped students understand societal expectations and see that their personal failures were not due to bad luck or not knowing the right people. She described how one of her inmate-students when, benefited from her ethics course for the first time in his life, he asked "the question if something was right or wrong" instead of asking "how do I get what I want."

Making Personal Transformations.   The prison culture created a discursive environment in which the educators learned to cope with and make sense of their new experiences with power, authority, and identity formation. This new understanding also helped them make personal transformations, which they described as positive. For example, when asked if teaching in the prison had changed her life, Gandalf replied, "I'm more tolerant, maybe. I never had really thought about inmates much." Kathryn and Seldom also stated that the experience of teaching in prison helped them develop a broader understanding of human nature. Seldom said, "Instead of narrowing [my] focus, it actually expanded it." Kathryn noted, "I didn't know how hungry they [inmate-students] really were to be good," and "I have a lot more insight and compassion for their [the prisoners'] struggle."

The physical proximity of these educators with their inmate-students may have encouraged them to feel more closely aligned with the inmates than with the prison officials, whom they rarely encountered. Although the educators with whom I spoke were not activists in prison reform, several of them described their inmate-students as multidimensional human beings with rights and not only as prisoners defined in terms of their deficiencies. For example, Kathryn explained how she began to recognize the many dimensions of her students while teaching college in a correctional facility for male youth offenders. She said, "What I find in them is the good part [and] the part that's really genuine starts to grow." As she constructed these young men as subjects rather than objects, she was resisting the Othering process, which marginalizes persons from a different race, gender, class, national origin, or sexual orientation.

It is also possible to realize in the stories of these educators how the personal becomes political. By sharing their subjective experiences, they were indirectly addressing social and political issues. The absence of organized social protest does not imply that the educators were not concerned about social problems that needed to be addressed. They seemed to use the research interviews as a space to elucidate their personal feelings regarding teaching college in prison and their stories became a vehicle for expressing their politics. Gandalf described how she had written to legislators in the mid-1990s to express her concern that the inmates were no longer eligible to receive Pell Grants for college courses. Seldom discussed how prison education reduced recidivism, which in turn reduced the cost of housing in prison and became an economic benefit for society.

Two Useful Conceptual Frameworks

Since we better understand educational practices using theories and models, I suggest two conceptual frameworks as lenses to help bring into sharper focus the experiences of community college educators who teach college in prison. First, the life-altering transition that educators make when they go inside prison walls to teach may be illuminated by reviewing Schlossberg's (1989) dichotomy of marginality and mattering. Second, Gubrium and Holstein's (2003) concept of discursive environments may provide an alternative context for appreciating the stories of these educators.

Marginality and Mattering.   Part-time faculty at community colleges and universities become involved and stay engaged with prison education for a variety of reasons. Schlossberg's (1989) polar themes of marginality and mattering may help explain how these prison educators feel both separate from and connected to their new environment. Schlossberg interviewed people in transition, who changed roles or experienced events that altered their lives. She found that the larger the difference between the former role and the new role, the greater the potential for feeling marginal. When educators go inside a prison to teach, they leave a familiar environment and enter the prison culture with no norms to anticipate their new role.

NEW DIRECTIONS FOR COMMUNITY COLLEGES • DOI: 10.1002/cc

In contrast to the theme of marginality, Schlossberg (1989) explored mattering, which she described as a "feeling that others depend on us, are interested in us, are concerned with our fate, or experience us as an ego-extension" (p. 8). Mattering can be a motivator and may determine behavior. For example, prison educators may be motivated to continue teaching in the prison environment because they feel they matter and make a difference in the lives of their inmate-students.

Discursive Environments and Multiple Identities.   Gubrium and Holstein (2003) noted that institutions shape our social life by creating an environment in which we "assemble, alter, and reformulate our lives" (p. 44). These environments are discursive because they provide distinctive ways for various participants to represent and interpret everyday life. In essence, hierarchical power relationships in these formal organizations alter the way their inhabitants view themselves and structure or reconfigure their personal identities in relation to others (Gubrium & Holstein, 2003). Similarly, Goffman (1958/1997) used the environments of total institutions to illustrate ways individuals develop understandings of who they are. Goffman's examples of total institutions include mental institutions, prisons, and military agencies that regulate all spheres of the individuals' lives under one roof and according to one rational plan with shared experiences and a common language.

The discursive environment of the prison setting allowed the educators in my study to make meaning of their unique experiences by constructing, reconstructing, and presenting multiple identities. In addition, the multiple roles that the prison system expects educators to play are a source of conflict and ambiguity (Wright, 2005). In contrast to their role as teachers, prison educators face institutional demands to act as prison guards to maintain security or as double agents to report back to prison authorities about undesirable behaviors of prisoners.

However, the prison educators with whom I spoke took advantage of public order and control to participate safely in another culture that is contradictory, frustrating, and occasionally dangerous. They frequently mentioned that the prison system was not designed for delivering high-quality educational programs because conditions of control conflicted with their goal to stimulate their students' intellectual curiosity and cognitive development. These educators learned to balance their personal values with the rules of the prison system, and they told stories of moving between being complicit with and countering the dominant prison culture. In their role as classroom teachers, these educators expressed their pleasure in sharing their passion for their area of expertise and in seeing the eagerness of their inmate-students to learn.

Furthermore, these educators had identities outside the prison, which they sometimes needed to balance with their identity of teaching in prison. These identities were formed through the participants' relationships with other people. The educators alternatively presented themselves as teachers outside the prison, students, spouses, parents, mentors, concerned citizens, social and political activists, researchers, and representatives of the world outside the prison walls. Finally, the educators saw themselves as strangers or adventurers who cross boundaries and enter into foreign culture.

Recommendations

Among their multiple missions and roles, community colleges provide special services to other publicly funded institutions (Cohen & Brawer, 1996). For example, many states contract with community colleges to provide basic skills and vocational training to inmates within their expanding prison system. While vocational training helps inmates develop skills for employment upon release, college courses in the tradition of liberal education promote self-awareness and self-esteem. One consideration is whether traditional college courses that include critical thinking and problem-solving skills should be replaced with programs that focus on occupational skills, good behaviors, and discipline (Chappell, 2004).

Prison education fits well with community colleges' commitment to providing low-cost access to higher education for all members of their communities. In the 1960s and 1970s, community colleges in Arizona, Maryland, Alabama, and Illinois provided basic skills and vocational training to inmates (Cohen & Brawer, 1996). In the following decade, these programs expanded to include associate degrees. Today, many colleges, universities, and nonprofit educational organizations partner with state correctional systems to offer college classes for credit.

For example, the Prison Teaching Initiative in New Jersey is a joint agreement by the state's Department of Corrections, Mercer County Community College (MCCC), and Princeton University to teach courses accredited by MCCC and to develop a degree-granting program. The College Bound Consortium is a pilot program administered by Drew University in partnership with Raritan Valley Community College to offer a joint associate and bachelor's degree program for students at New Jersey's only state prison for women. In New York, the Cornell Prison Education Program is a collaboration among the New York State Department of Corrections, Cornell University, and Cayuga Community College to bring free college education to inmates in a medium and maximum security facility near Ithaca, New York.

In October 2010, Education Justice Project at the University of Illinois hosted a symposium on higher education in prison. The presenters included representatives from college-in-prison programs from across the United States to discuss their programs and develop strategies for action. Additionally, Education from the Inside Out Coalition, a New York–based collaborative of criminal justice and education advocates, is working to remove barriers to higher education funding facing students in prisons nationwide. One of the coalition's goals is to lobby for the restoration of

Pell Grant eligibility of prisoners, which would reflect the original legislative intent of providing need-based grants to all low-income students.

Community colleges should use these examples of good practices if they plan to add prison higher education to their programs. Furthermore, community college educators and administrators should consider joining the efforts to lift the prohibition of using Pell Grants for prisoners to gain access to higher education before their release.

Conclusion

The frequent argument to justify future funding of college programs in prisons is that they can contribute to a range of positive outcomes. These constructive results include reducing recidivism and increasing employability of released prisoners (Lawrence, Mears, Dubin, & Travis, 2002; Taylor, 1994). Furthermore, most prison administrators acknowledge that prisoners enrolled in college courses commit fewer infractions of prison rules, which saves time and money for the prison system (Baust, McWilliams, Murray, & Schmidt, 2006).

In fact, the penal code in most states expresses the goal of rehabilitation of the prisoners so that they may become productive members of society upon release (Taylor, 1994). However, the current rapid growth of the prison population coupled with constraints on prison budgets presents barriers to implementing and operating educational programs in correctional settings. As Torre and Fine (2005) noted, "Prisoners may, at the present historical moment, be the only group of U.S. citizens systematically barred from public support for access to higher education" (p. 570).

This chapter began by applying the metaphor of "stranger" to prison educators. As mainly part-time faculty members hired by local colleges and universities to teach academic courses in prison, they become outsiders in both the higher educational community and in the correctional system. Through their stories from the borderland, the prison educators in my study described feeling marginal yet they believed they were central to the lives of their inmate-students. As the prison population continues to grow, community colleges can play an important role in providing access to a college education for those students behind bars and offer an enriching experience for participating educators.

References

Baust, D. C., McWilliams, A. P., Murray, B. M., & Schmidt, K. G. *College for the incarcerated: Funding alternatives for Maryland post-secondary correctional education.* Baltimore, MD: University of Maryland-Baltimore County, Shriver Center. http://shrivercenter.org/documents/gsip_policy_papers2006/College%20for%20the%20Incarcerated.pdf, 2006.
Chappell, C. A. Post-secondary correctional education and recidivism: A meta-analysis of research conducted 1990–1999. *Journal of Correctional Education,* 2004, 55(2), 148–169.

Cohen, A. M., & Brawer, F. B. *The American community college* (3rd ed.). San Francisco, CA: Jossey-Bass, 1996.

Edwards, F. M. Behind the open door: Disadvantaged students. In A. Levine (Ed.), *Higher learning in America: 1980–2000*. Baltimore, MD: Johns Hopkins University Press, 1993.

Eggleston, C., & Gehring, T. Democracy in prison and prison education. *Journal of Correctional Education,* 2000, *51*(3), 306–310.

Erisman, W., & Contardo, J. B. *Learning to reduce recidivism: A 50-state analysis of postsecondary correctional education policy.* Washington, DC: Institute for Higher Education Policy, 2005.

Goffman, E. The mortified self: The characteristics of total institutions. In C. Lemert & A. Branaman (Eds.), *The Goffman reader.* Malden, MA: Blackwell, 1997. [Originally published in 1958 and copyrighted in 1961.].

Gubrium, J. F., & Holstein, J. A. From the individual interview to the interview society. In J. F. Gubrium & J. A. Holstein (Eds.), *Postmodern interviewing*. Thousand Oaks, CA: Sage, 2003.

Lawrence, S., Mears, D., Dubin, G., & Travis, J. *The practice and promise of prison programming*. Washington, DC: Urban Institute, Justice Policy Center's Research for Safer Communities, 2002.

Linebaugh, P. Freeing birds, erasing images, burning lamps: How I learned to teach in prison. In H. S. Davidson (Ed.), *Schooling in a "total institution": Critical perspectives on prison education*. Westport, CT: Bergin & Garvey, 1995.

Roueche, J. E., Roueche, S. D., & Milliron, M. D. *Strangers in their own land: Part-time faculty in American community colleges*. Washington, DC: Community College Press, 1995.

Schlossberg, N. K. Marginality and mattering: Key issues in building community. *New Directions for Student Services*, 1989, *48*, 5–15.

Silva, W. A brief history of prison higher education in the United States. In M. Williford (Ed.), *Higher education in prison: A contradiction in terms?* Phoenix, AZ: Oryx Press, 1994.

Spaulding, S. B. A bricolage of narratives about teaching college in prison: Interpreting through a performance text. PhD dissertation, Colorado State University, 1994.

Taylor, J. M. Should prisoners have access to collegiate education? A policy issue. *Educational Policy*, 2008, *8*(3), 315–338.

Tewksbury, R., Erickson, D. J., & Taylor, J. M. Opportunities lost: The consequences of eliminating Pell Grant eligibility for correctional education students. *Journal of Offender Rehabilitation*, 2000, *31*(1/2), 43–56.

Torre, M. E., & Fine, M. Bar none: Extending affirmative action to higher education in prison. *Journal of Social Issues*, 2005, *61*(3), 569–594.

Weiss, L., & Fine, M. *Working method: Research and social justice*. New York, NY: Routledge, 2004.

Wright, R. Teacher burnout and toxic cultures in alternative school/prison settings. *Journal of Juvenile Court, Community and Alternative School Administrators of California*, 2005, *18*, 44–53.

Wright, R. Metaphors of experience: The prison teacher as stranger. In R. Wright (Ed.), *In the borderlands: Learning to teach in prisons and alternative settings*. Elkridge, MD: Correctional Education Association, 2006.

SUSANNA SPAULDING is an associate professor of entrepreneurship at Colorado Mountain College. She was formerly the director of a community college academic center and managed a college program in a medium- and minimum-security prison.

NEW DIRECTIONS FOR COMMUNITY COLLEGES • DOI: 10.1002/cc

This chapter provides resources to assist student affairs personnel at community colleges as they interact with students from marginalized groups, students whose experiences in college need to be heard and brought to the center. The resources described are practice oriented and include Web links of professional organizations with further sources of information for each particular marginalized group. Funding opportunities are also identified to help further support community colleges' ability to program, recruit, and retain these marginalized populations. The goal of each community college to serve all students will largely depend on the willingness of administrators, faculty, and staff to critique and confront why certain student groups remain on the margins of their respective campuses.

Key Resources on Marginalized Students

Susana Hernandez, Ignacio Hernandez

LGBT Students on Community College Campuses

The recent spate of tragic suicides of LGBT persons is cause for alarm and reason for college personnel to be conscious of their campus culture. More important, it should be a call to action to shed light on the marginalized intersection of oppressed identities of gay students in American society.

Gay, Lesbian, and Straight Education Network (GLSEN). GLSEN seeks to develop school climates where difference is valued for the positive contribution it makes in creating a more vibrant and diverse community. Anyone, regardless of sexual orientation, gender identity/expression, or occupation, who is committed to seeing this philosophy realized in school settings, may become involved in supporting the organization's mission. While serving on a national scale, local chapters receive guidance from the national office and are run mostly on a volunteer basis. Further information may be accessed online at www.glsen.org, by calling 212-727-0135, or by e-mail at glsen@glsen.org.

Student Affairs Administrators in Higher Education (NASPA)— Gay, Lesbian, Bisexual, and Transgender (GLBT) Issues Knowledge Community. This national professional organization promotes a Gay,

Lesbian, and Transgender Knowledge Community in which student affairs professionals can obtain more information and resources about this community. In particular, the knowledge community shares knowledge and community activities that facilitate personal and professional development opportunities. www.naspa.org/kc/glbt/default.cfm

American College Personnel Association (ACPA)—Standing Committee for Lesbian, Gay, Bisexual, and Transgender Awareness (SCLGBTA). The goals of the SCLGBTA are to educate the general membership of ACPA in order to increase their personal and environmental awareness of the social, psychological, health-related, political, economic, professional, legal, and spiritual realities of lesbian, gay, bisexual, and transgender persons. Their web site hosts a number of additional resources for student affairs professionals working with this community. www.myacpa.org/sc/sclgbta/index.cfm

Related Reading. Sanlo, R. L. (Ed.). (2005). Gender identity and sexual orientation: Research, policy, and personal perspectives. *New Directions for Student Services*, No. 111. San Francisco, CA: Jossey-Bass.

This special issue provides a rich literature for those seeking ways to support lesbian, gay, bisexual, and transgender college students. The volume describes research, policies, and current issues for LGBT students and faculty, but we want to bring special attention to Brian T. Ivory's chapter, *LGBT Students in Community College: Characteristics, Challenges, and Recommendations,* which discusses community college students in particular.

Funding Opportunity. Guilford Green Foundation: www.ggfnc.org/grants.html

Student Athletes

Community College Counselors/Advisors Academic Association for Athletes (3c4a). 3c4a is an organization established in the state of California whose purpose is to bring together individuals who provide academic counseling, advisement, and assistance for student athletes at the community college level. www.3c4a.org/

National Junior College Athletic Association (NJCAA). The NJCAA is the governing body of intercollegiate athletics for two-year colleges. Its programs are designed to meet the unique needs of a diverse group of student-athletes whose purpose in selecting a two-year college may be as varied as their experiences before attending college. www.njcaa.org/

This link is from the NCAA and specifically addresses the achievement gap faced by student athletes who transfer from a community college to a four-year institution. www.ncaa.org/wps/wcm/connect/ncaa/ncaa/ncaa+news/ncaa+news+online/2010/division+i/di_working_to_solve_two_year_transfer_riddle_05_10_10

Related Reading. Howard-Hamilton, M. F., & Watt, S. K. (Eds.). Student services for athletes. *New Directions for Student Services*, No. 93. San Francisco, CA: Jossey-Bass, 2001.

This special issue in the *New Directions* series is directed at student services and athletic administrators looking for better ways to include the student athlete into the mainstream of college student experiences. The authors expressly seek to help student affairs personnel create programs and policies to foster student athletes' learning and development both in and out of the classroom. Broughton and Neyer's chapter suggests an advising and counseling model for student athletes beyond the traditional issues of academic eligibility and graduation rates, which may often further marginalize the student athlete. Readers of the chapter may include this resource as a way of evaluating their approach to working with this student population.

Academically Underprepared Students

National Academic Advising Association (NACADA). NACADA (www.nacada.ksu.edu/) promotes and supports quality academic advising in institutions of higher education to enhance the educational development of students. NACADA provides a clearinghouse of links addressing academically underprepared students in college. Further information may be accessed online by visiting www.nacada.ksu.edu/Clearinghouse/AdvisingIssues /Academically-Underprepared.htm.

Related Reading. Gabriel, K. F. (2008). *Teaching unprepared students: Strategies for promoting success and retention in higher education*. Sterling, VA: Stylus.

This book provides a practical guide for faculty and staff working with academically underprepared students including techniques and approaches that can be implemented to create positive conditions and a campus environment that supports this marginalized student population.

Funding Opportunity. Bill and Melinda Gates Foundation— Postsecondary Education Grants: www.gatesfoundation.org/grantseeker /Pages/funding-postsecondary-education.aspx

Veterans

United States Department of Veterans Affairs. As more student veterans transition from war zones to college campuses, higher education personnel must begin to understand their transition experience. Following is a list of some useful resources in understanding the policies that govern the GI Bill as well as professional organizations for educators.

The United States Office of Veterans Affairs coordinates and manages the GI Bill. Educators and veterans can locate eligible schools, apply for the GI Bill, and find information on a host of other resources at www.gibill .va.gov/.

NEW DIRECTIONS FOR COMMUNITY COLLEGES • DOI: 10.1002/cc

National Association of Veterans Programs Administrators (NAVPA).   NAVPA's main purpose is to promote professional competency and efficiency through an association of members and others associated with, and involved in, veterans educational programs; to promote the development, improvement, and extension of opportunities to any veteran or dependent of a veteran. Further information may be accessed at www .navpa.org/.

Council of College and Military Educators (CCME).   The membership is composed of military educators, civilian educators, postsecondary educational institutions, and suppliers of quality education products and services. The CCME's mission is to promote and provide educational programs and services as well as to facilitate communication between the membership and the Department of Defense educational support network. www.ccmeonline.org/ccme.aspx

Related Reading.   Ackerman, R., & DiRamio, D. (Eds.). Supporting student veterans in transition: Creating a veteran-friendly campus: Strategies for transition success. *New Directions for Student Services*, No. 126. San Francisco, CA: Jossey-Bass, 2009.

This special issue in the *New Directions for Student Services* series is dedicated to the timely issue of transitions related to combat veterans enrolling in college campuses. In the chapters, the reader will hear from contributors who work to understand the needs of students who are making the transition from military service, have participated in the development of programs in response to those needs, or have themselves experienced the transition from the military to the campus.

Noncredit ESL

National Council of Teachers of English (NCTE).   The NCTE has released a position paper and a policy brief on English language learners. Information can be accessed via the NCTE web site: www.ncte.org/ell.

Community College Consortium of Immigrant Education (CCCIE). The CCCIE's mission is to raise awareness of the important role community colleges play in delivering educational opportunities to immigrants and to promote and expand the range and quality of programs and services for immigrant students among community colleges around the country. The consortium web site provides a list of additional resources as well as promising practices of existing community college programs. www .sunywcc.edu

Related Reading.   Chisman, F. P., & Crandall, J. (2007). *Passing the torch: Strategies for innovation in community college ESL.* New York, NY: Council for the Advancement of Adult Literacy.

This report is sponsored by the Council for the Advancement of Adult Literacy and is the result of a national study of noncredit ESL programs in community colleges across the United States. The report examines and highlights innovative programs and strategies used in exemplary ESL programs and instruction.

Funding Opportunity. United States Department of Education-Office of English Language Acquisition: www2.ed.gov/about/offices/list/oela/funding.html

Students in Prison

Correctional Education Association (CEA). The CEA is the nonprofit professional association serving educators and administrators who provide services to students in correctional settings. Their web site offers a variety of resources for educators working with students in correctional settings or those seeking release and transition to traditional educational settings. www.ceanational.org/index2.htm

Office of Correctional Education. The Office of Correctional Education is part of the Department of Education (ED) and is housed under the Office of Vocational and Adult Education. Resources on their web site include a corrections research library, government funding programs, and demonstration projects that may serve as templates for educators. www2.ed.gov/offices/OVAE/AdultEd/OCE/index.html

North Carolina Department of Corrections. North Carolina's Department of Corrections employs an educational services office that offers inmates education activities "so that they may become responsible and productive persons who can effectively manage their incarceration and make contributions to their community upon release." The Department of Corrections jointly develops its education programs with the North Carolina Community College System (NCCCS). The Department of Corrections and the NCCCS meet twice a year to convene an interagency committee to guide educational policies. Annual reports and periodic newsletters can be accessed through their web site. www.doc.state.nc.us/dop/education/index.htm

Funding Opportunity. United States Office of Correctional Education Grants: www2.ed.gov/offices/OVAE/AdultEd/OCE/funding.html

SUSANA HERNANDEZ is a doctoral student in the Department of Educational Leadership and Policy Studies at Iowa State University in Ames, Iowa.

IGNACIO HERNANDEZ is a doctoral student and research associate in the Community College Leadership Program at Iowa State University.

INDEX